Translation and Multilingual Natural Language Processing

Chief Editor: Reinhard Rapp (Johannes Gutenberg-Universität Mainz)
Consulting Editors: Silvia Hansen-Schirra, Oliver Čulo (Johannes Gutenberg-Universität Mainz)

In this series:

1. Fantinuoli, Claudio & Federico Zanettin (eds.). New directions in corpus-based translation studies

New directions in corpus-based translation studies

Edited by

Claudio Fantinuoli and Federico Zanettin

language
science
press

Claudio Fantinuoli and Federico Zanettin (ed.). 2015. *New directions in corpus-based translation studies* (Translation and Multilingual Natural Language Processing 1). Berlin: Language Science Press.

This title can be downloaded at:
http://langsci-press.org/catalog/book/76
© 2015, the authors
Published under the Creative Commons Attribution 4.0 Licence (CC BY 4.0):
http://creativecommons.org/licenses/by/4.0/
ISBN: 978-3-944675-83-1

Cover and concept of design: Ulrike Harbort
Typesetting: Claudio Fantinuoli, Katrin Hamberger, Felix Kopecky, Sebastian Nordhoff
Proofreading: Željko Agić, Benedikt Baur, Rachele De Felice, Stefan Hartmann, Rebekah Ingram, Ka Shing Ko, Kristina Pelikan, Christian Pietsch, Daniela Schröder, Charlotte van Tongeren
Fonts: Linux Libertine, Arimo
Typesetting software:

Language Science Press
Habelschwerdter Allee 45
14195 Berlin, Germany
langsci-press.org

Storage and cataloguing done by FU Berlin

Freie Universität Berlin

Contents

Chapter 1

Creating and using multilingual corpora in translation studies
Claudio Fantinuoli and Federico Zanettin

1 Introduction

Corpus linguistics has become a major paradigm and research methodology in translation theory and practice, with practical applications ranging from professional human translation to machine (assisted) translation and terminology. Corpus-based theoretical and descriptive research has investigated written and interpreted language, and topics such as translation universals and norms, ideology and individual translator style (Laviosa 2002; Olohan 2004; Zanettin 2012), while corpus-based tools and methods have entered the curricula at translation training institutions (Zanettin, Bernardini & Stewart 2003; Beeby, Rodríguez Inés & Sánchez-Gijón 2009). At the same time, taking advantage of advancements in terms of computational power and increasing availability of electronic texts, enormous progress has been made in the last 20 years or so as regards the development of applications for professional translators and machine translation system users (Coehn 2009; Brunette 2013).

The contributions to this volume, which are centred around seven European languages (Basque, Dutch, German, Greek, Italian, Spanish and English), add to the range of studies of corpus-based descriptive studies, and provide examples of some less explored applications of corpus analysis methods to translation research. The chapters, which are based on papers first presented at the 7th congress of the European Society of Translation Studies held in Germersheim in

Claudio Fantinuoli & Federico Zanettin. 2014. Creating and using multilingual corpora in translation studies. In Claudio Fantinuoli & Federico Zanettin (eds.), *New directions in corpus-based translation studies*, 1–10. Berlin: Language Science Press

July/August 2013[1], encompass a variety of research aims and methodologies, and vary as concerns corpus design and compilation, and the techniques used to analyze the data. Corpus-based research in descriptive translation studies critically depends on the availability of suitable tools and resources, and most articles in this volume focus on the creation of corpus resources which were not formerly available, and which, once created, will hopefully provide a basis for further research.

The first article, by Tatiana Serbina, Paula Niemietz and Stella Neumann, proposes a novel approach to the study of the translation process, which merges process and product data. The authors describe the development of a bilingual parallel translation corpus in which source texts and translations are aligned together with a record of the actions carried out by translators, for instance by inserting or deleting a character, clicking the mouse, or highlighting a segment of text. The second article, by Effie Mouka, Ioannis Saridakis and Angeliki Fotopoulou, is an attempt at using corpus techniques to implement a critical discourse approach to the analysis of translation based on Appraisal Theory. The authors describe the development of a trilingual parallel corpus of English, Greek and Spanish film subtitles, and the analysis focuses on racist discourse. The third article, by Naroa Zubillaga, Zuriñe Sanz and Ibon Uribarri, describes the developments of a trilingual parallel corpus of German, Basque and Spanish literary texts. Spanish texts, which were included when used as relay texts for translating from German into Basque, provide a means for the study of translation directness. In the following article Ekaterina Lapshinova-Koltunski uses a corpus which contains translations of the same source texts carried out using different methods of translation, namely, human, computer aided and fully automated. Her chapter provides an innovative contribution to the description of systematic variation in terms of translation features. Steven Doms investigates the strategies translators use to translate non-human agents in subject position when working from English into Dutch. Finally, Gianluca Pontrandolfo's study addresses the needs of practicing and training legal translators by proposing a trilingual comparable phraseological repertoire, based on COSPE, a 6-million word corpus of Spanish, Italian and English criminal judgments.

Rather than providing a summary of the articles, for which individual abstracts are available, we have chosen to briefly illustrate some of the issues involved in different stages of corpus construction and use as exemplified in the case studies included in this volume.

---

[1] All selected articles have undergone a rigorous double blind peer reviewing process, each being assessed by two reviewers.

2 Corpus design

The initial thrust to descriptive corpus-based studies (CBS) in translation came in the 1990s, when researchers and scholars saw in large corpora of monolingual texts an opportunity to further a target oriented approach to the study of translation, based on the systemic comparison and contrast between translated and non-translated texts in the target language (Baker 1993). In the wake of the first studies based on the Translation English Corpus (TEC) (Laviosa 1997) various other corpora of translated texts were compiled and used in conjunction with comparable corpora of non-translated texts. Descriptive translation research using multilingual corpora progressed more slowly, primarily because of lack of suitable resources. Pioneering projects such as the English Norwegian Parallel Corpus (ENPC), set up in the 1990s under the guidance of Stig Johansson (see e.g. Johansson 2007) and later expanded into the Oslo Multilingual Corpus, which involved more than one language and issues of bitextual annotation and alignment, were a productive source of studies in contrastive linguistics and translation, but they were not easily replicable because the creation of such resources is more time consuming and technically complex than that of monolingual corpora.[2] Thus, research was initially mostly restricted to small scale projects, often involving a single text pair, and non re-usable resources. However, the last few years have seen the development of some robust multilingual and parallel corpus projects, which can and have been used as resources in a number of descriptive translation studies. Two of these corpora, the Dutch Parallel Corpus (Rura, Vandeweghe & Perez 2008) and the German-English CroCo Corpus (Hansen-Schirra, Neumann & Steiner 2013) are in fact sources of data for two of the articles contained in this volume. Other corpora used in the studies in this volume were instead newly created as re-usable resources.

Typically, a distinction is made between (bi- or multi-lingual) parallel corpora, said to contain source and target texts, and comparable corpora, defined as corpora created according to similar design criteria. However, not only is the terminology somewhat unstable (Zanettin 2012: 149) but the distinction between the two types of corpora is not always clear cut. First, parallel corpora do not

---

[2] Given the advances in parallel corpus processing behind developments in statistical machine translations, it may appear somewhat surprising that they have not benefited descriptive research more decisively. However, while descriptive and pedagogic research depends on manual analysis and requires data of high quality, research in statistical machine translation privileges automation and data quantity, and thus tools and data developed for machine translation (including alignment techniques and tools, and aligned data), are usually not suitable or available for descriptive translation studies research.

necessarily contain translations. For instance, the largest multilingual parallel corpora publicly available, Europarl and Acquis Communautaire, created by the activity of European Institutions, contain all originals in a legal sense. Second, comparable corpora may have varying degrees of similarity and contain not only "original" texts but also translations. Third, various "hybrid texts" exist in which "translated" text is intermingled with "comparable" text, very similar in terms of subject matter, register etc., but not a translation which can be traced to "parallel" source text. Examples include news translation and text crowdsourcing (e.g. Wikipedia articles in multiple languages), which are generated through "transediting" (Stetting 1989) practices and are thus partly "original writing" and partly translation, possibly from multiple sources.

It may thus be useful to consider the attribute "parallel" or "comparable" as referring to a type of corpus architecture, rather than to the status of the texts as concerns translation. Parallel corpora can thus be thought of as corpora in which two or more components are aligned, that is, are subdivided into compositional and sequential units (of differing extent and nature) which are linked and can thus be retrieved as pairs (or triplets, etc.). On the other hand, comparable corpora can be thought of as corpora which are compared on the whole on the basis of assumed similarity.

A distinctive feature of the corpora described in this volume is their complexity, as most corpora contain more than two subcorpora, often in different languages, and in some cases together with different types of data. Serbina, Niemietz and Neumann's keystroke logged corpus contains original texts and translations, together with the intermediate versions of the unfolding translation process. The corpus is based on keystroke logging and eye-tracking data recorded during translation, editing and post-editing experiments. The log of keystrokes is seen as an intermediate version between source and final translation. The corpus created by Mouka, Saridakis and Fotopoulou is a multilingual and multimodal corpus comprising five films in English together with English, Greek and Spanish subtitles. The films were selected for their related subject matter and contain a significant amount of conversation carried out in interracial communities, and feature several instances of racist discourse. Zubillaga, Sanz and Uribarri describe the design and compilation of Aleuska, a multilingual parallel corpus of translations from German to Basque. The corpus, which collates three subcorpora of literary and philosophical texts, was collected after meticulous bibliographic research. Translation into a minority language, such as Basque, is a complex phenomenon, and this complexity is reflected in the design of the corpus, which includes a subcorpus of Spanish texts used as a relay language in the translation process.

Lapshinova-Koltunski's VARiation in TRAnslation (VARTRA) corpus comprises five sets of translations of the same source texts carried out using different translation methods, together with the source texts and a set of comparable German originals. The first subcorpus of translations is a selection extracted from the Cross-linguistic Corpus (CroCo) (Hansen-Schirra, Neumann & Steiner 2013), which contains human translations together with their source texts from various registers of written language. Since CroCo is a bidirectional corpus, it also contains a set of comparable source texts in German (and their English translations, which however were not needed for this investigation). The second set of German translations contains texts produced by translators with the help of Computer Assisted Translation (CAT) tools, while each of the three remaining subcorpora contains the output of a different machine translation system. The last two articles in this collection focus on corpus analysis rather than on the design and construction of the corpora used, which are described extensively elsewhere. However, it is clear that results are as good as the criteria which guided the creation of the corpora from which they are derived. Doms draws his data from the Dutch Parallel Corpus (DPC), a balanced 10 million word corpus of English, French and Dutch originals and translations, while the data analyzed by Pontrandolfo come from the COrpus de Sentencias PEnales (COSPE), a carefully constructed specialized corpus of legal discourse. COSPE is a trilingual comparable corpus and does not contain translations, though its Italian, English and Spanish subcorpora are extremely similar from the point of view of domain, genre and register.

3 Annotation and alignment

The enrichment of a corpus with linguistic and extra-linguistic annotation may play a decisive part in descriptive studies based on corpora of translations, and are of particular concern to the first four articles, in which research implementation relies to a large extent on annotation. Issues of annotation and alignment come to the fore in the study by Sebine, Niemetz and Neumann, who show how both process and product data can be annotated in XML format in order to query the corpus for various features and recurring patterns. The keylogged data provided by the Translog software are pre-processed to represent individual keystroke logging events as linguistic structures, and these process units are then aligned with source and target text units. All process data, even material that does not appear in the final translation product, is preserved, under the assumption that all intermediate steps are meaningful to an understanding of the translation process.

Bringing together approaches from descriptive translation studies and critical discourse linguistics, Mouka, Saridakis and Fotopoulou address the topic of racism in multimedia translation by creating a time-aligned corpus of film dialogues, and attempting to code and classify instances of racist discourse in English subtitles and their translations in multiple languages. The authors devise a taxonomy of racism-related utterances in the light of Appraisal Theory (Martin & White 2005), and use the ELAN and GATE applications to apply multiple layers of XML, TEI conformant annotation to the multimodal and multilingual corpus. Racism-related utterances in the source and target languages are classified in order to allow for the analysis of register shifts in translation. The subtitles are aligned together into the trilingual parallel corpus as well as synchronized with the audiovisual data, allowing access to the wider context for every utterance retrieved.

Zubillaga, Sanz and Uribarri had to face the challenge of working with a minority language, Basque, for which scarce computational linguistics resources are available, and had therefore to develop their own tools. Research into literary translations from German into Basque involves direct translations from German into Basque but also indirect translation, carried out by going through a Spanish version. In order to observe both texts in the case of direct translations and all three texts for indirect translations, Zubillaga, Sanz and Uribarri have aligned their XML annotated parallel trilingual corpus at sentence level, using a project specific alignment tool.

The features chosen for comparative analysis in Lapshinova-Koltunski's chapter were obtained on the basis of automatic linguistic annotation. All subcorpora were tokenised, lemmatised, tagged with part of speech information, and segmented into syntactic chunks and sentences, and were then encoded in a format compatible with the IMS Open Corpus Workbench corpus management and query tool. Though the set of translations extracted from the CroCo corpus are aligned with their source texts, the five subcorpora of translations are not aligned between them since this annotation level is not necessary for the extraction of the operationalisations used in this study. In this respect, then, VARTRA is treated as a comparable rather than as a parallel corpus.

Dom's data are a collection of parallel concordances drawn from the Dutch Parallel Corpus, and annotation and alignment at sentence level are clearly prerequisites for the type of investigation conducted. Pontrandolfo's COSPE contains criminal judgements in different languages by different judicial systems, and therefore the texts in the three subcorpora cannot be aligned. However, as shown by Pontrandolfo, both researchers and translators can benefit from research based on corpora which are neither linguistically annotated nor aligned.

4 Corpus analysis

Sebine, Niemetz and Neumann offer several examples of possible data queries and discuss how linguistically informed quantitative analyses of the translation process data can be performed. They show how the analysis of the intermediate versions of the unfolding text during the translation process can be used to trace the development of the linguistic phenomena found in the final product. Mouka, Saridakis and Fotopoulou use the apparatus of systemic-functional linguistics to trace register shifts in instances of racist discourse in films translated from English into Greek and Spanish. They also avail themselves of large comparable monolingual corpora in English and Greek as a backdrop against which to evaluate original and translated utterances in their corpus. Zubillaga, Sanz and Uribarri provide a preliminary exploration of the type of searches that can be performed using the Aleuska corpus using the accompanying search engine. They frame their search hypothesis within Toury's (1995) translation laws, finding evidence both of standardisation and interference, in direct as well as in indirect translation.

Lapshinova-Koltunski's chapter is one of the first investigations which compares corpora obtained through different methods of translation to test a theoretical hypothesis rather than to evaluate the performance of machine translation systems. The subcorpora are queried using regular expressions based on part of speech annotation which retrieve words belonging to specific word classes or phrase types. These lexicogrammatical patterns, together with word count statistics, are used as indicators of four hypothesized translation specific features, namely simplification, explicitation, normalisation vs. "shining through", and convergence. While these features have been amply investigated in the literature, the novelty of Lapshinova-Koltunski's study is that the comparison takes into account not only variation between translated and non-translated texts, but also with respect to the method of translation. Preliminary results show interesting patterns of variation for the features under analysis.

Doms analyses 338 parallel concordances containing instances of the English verbs *give* and *show* with an agent as their subject, and their Dutch translations. The analysis was carried out manually by filtering out from search results unwanted instances such as passive and idiomatic constructions, and by distinguishing between human and non-human agents. First, the author provides a discussion of the prototypical features of agents which perform the action with particular verbs, and an overview of the different constraints which certain verbs pose on the use of human and non-human agents in English and Dutch, respectively.

He then zooms in on the two verbs under analysis, and discusses the data from the corpus. Since sentences with action verbs like *give* or *show* and non-human agents are less frequently attested in Dutch than in English, the expectation is that translators will not (always) translate English non-human agents as subjects of *give* and *show* with Dutch non-human agents as subjects of the Dutch cognates of *give* and *show*, *geven* and *tonen*, respectively. Doms describes the choices made by the translators both on a syntactic and semantic level, comparing the translation data with the source-text sentences to verify whether these source-text verbs give rise to different solutions, showing how the translators decided between either primed translations with non-human agents and translations without non-human agents, but with specific Dutch syntactic and semantic patterns which differ from those in the English source texts.

Pontrandolfo presents the results of an empirical study of LSP phraseological units in a specific domain (criminal law) and type of legal genre (criminal judgments), approaching contrastive phraseology both from a quantitative and a qualitative perspective. He describes how four categories of phraseological units, namely complex prepositions, lexical doublets and triplets, lexical collocations and routine formulae, were extracted from the corpus using a mix of manual and automatic techniques. He shows how formulaic language, which plays a pivotal role in judicial discourse, can be analyzed and compared across three languages by means of concordancing software. The final goal of Pontrandolfo's research is to provide a resource for legal translators, as well as for legal experts, which can help them develop their phraseological competence through exposure to real, authentic (con)texts in which these phraseological units are used.

5 Conclusions

Corpus-based translation studies have steadily grown as a disciplinary sub-category since the first studies began to appear more than twenty years ago. A bibliometric analysis of data extracted from the Translation Studies Abstracts Online database shows that in the last ten years or so about 1 out of 10 publications in the field has been concerned with or informed by corpus linguistics methods (Zanettin, Saldanha & Harding 2015). The contributions to this volume show that the area keeps evolving, as it constantly opens up to different frameworks and approaches, from Appraisal Theory to process-oriented analysis, and encompasses multiple translation settings, including (indirect) literary translation, machine (assisted)-translation and the practical work of professional legal translators (and interpreters). Finally, the studies included in the volume expand the range of application of corpus applications not only in terms of corpus design and methodologies, but also in terms of the tools used to accomplish the research tasks outlined. Corpus-based research critically depends on the availability of suitable tools and resources, and in order to cope properly with the challenges posed by increasingly complex and varied research settings, generally available data sources and out of the box software can be usefully complemented by tools tailored to the needs of specific research purposes. In this sense, a stronger tie between technical expertise and sound methodological practice may be key to exploring new directions in corpus-based translation studies.

References

Baker, Mona. 1993. Corpus linguistics and translation studies: Implications and applications. In Mona Baker, Gill Francis & Elena Tognini-Bonelli (eds.), *Text and technology: In honour of John Sinclair*, 233–250. Amsterdam: John Benjamins.

Beeby, Allison, Patricia Rodríguez Inés & Pilar Sánchez-Gijón. 2009. *Corpus use and translating: Corpus use for learning to translate and learning corpus use to translate*. Amsterdam: John Benjamins.

Brunette, Louise. 2013. Machine translation and the working methods of translators. *Special issue of JosTrans* (19). 2–7.

Coehn, Philipp. 2009. *Statistical machine translation*. Cambridge: Cambridge University Press.

Hansen-Schirra, Silvia, Stella Neumann & Erich Steiner. 2013. *Cross-linguistic corpora for the study of translations. Insights from the language pair English-German*. Berlin: de Gruyter.

Johansson, Stig. 2007. *Seeing through multilingual corpora: On the use of corpora in contrastive studies*. Amsterdam: John Benjamins.

Laviosa, Sara. 1997. How comparable can "comparable corpora" be? *Target* 9(2). 289–319.

Laviosa, Sara. 2002. *Corpus-based translation studies: Theory, findings, applications*. Amsterdam: Rodopi.

Martin, James Robert & Peter R. R. White. 2005. *The language of evaluation: Appraisal in English*. London: Palgrave Macmillan.

Olohan, Maeve. 2004. *Introducing corpora in translation studies*. London: Routledge.

Rura, Lidia, Willy Vandeweghe & Maribel M. Perez. 2008. Designing a parallel corpus as a multifunctional translator's aid. In *Proceedings of the XVIII FIT World Congress*. Shanghai.

Stetting, Karen. 1989. Transediting – A new term for coping with the grey area between editing and translating. In Graham Caie, Kirsten Haastrup & Arnt Lykke Jakobsen (eds.), *Proceedings from the fourth nordic conference for english studies*, 371–382. Copenhagen: University of Copenhagen.

Toury, Gideon. 1995. *Descriptive translation studies and beyond*. Amsterdam: John Benjamins.

Zanettin, Federico. 2012. *Translation-driven corpora: Corpus resources for descriptive and applied translation studies*. Manchester: St. Jerome Publishing.

Zanettin, Federico, Silvia Bernardini & Dominic Stewart (eds.). 2003. *Corpora in translator education*. Manchester: St. Jerome Publishing.

Zanettin, Federico, Gabriela Saldanha & Sue-Ann Harding. 2015. Sketching landscapes in translation studies. A bibliographic study. *Perspectives: Studies in Translatology* 23(2). 1–22.

Chapter 2

Development of a keystroke logged translation corpus

Tatiana Serbina, Paula Niemietz and Stella Neumann

This paper describes the development of a keystroke logged translation corpus containing both translation product and process data. The initial data comes from a translation experiment and contains original texts and translations, plus the intermediate versions of the unfolding translation process. The aim is to annotate both process and product data to be able to query for various features and recurring patterns. However, the data must first be pre-processed to represent individual keystroke logging events as linguistic structures, and align source, target and process units. All process data, even material that does not appear in the final translation product, is preserved, under the assumption that all intermediate steps are meaningful to our understanding of the translation process. Several examples of possible data queries are discussed to show how linguistically informed quantitative analyses of the translation process data can be performed.

1 Introduction

Empirical translation studies can be subdivided into two main branches, namely product and process-based investigations (see Laviosa 2002; Göpferich 2008). Traditionally, the former are associated with corpus studies, while the latter require translation experiments. The present study combines these two perspectives on translation by treating the translation process data as a corpus and tracing how linguistic phenomena found in the final product have developed during the translation process.

Typically, product-based studies consider translations as texts in their own right, which can be analyzed in terms of translation properties, i.e. ways in which translated texts systematically differ from the originals. The main translation

Tatiana Serbina, Paula Niemietz & Stella Neumann. 2014. Development of a keystroke logged translation corpus. In Claudio Fantinuoli & Federico Zanettin (eds.), *New directions in corpus-based translation studies*, 11–31. Berlin: Language Science Press properties analyzed so far include simplification, explicitation, normalization towards the target text (TT), leveling out (Baker 1996) and shining through of the source text (ST) (Teich 2003). Investigations into these properties can be conducted using monolingual comparable corpora containing originals and translations within the same language (e.g. Laviosa 2002), bilingual parallel corpora consisting of originals and their aligned translations (e.g. Becher 2010), or also combinations of both (Čulo et al. 2012; Hansen-Schirra & Steiner 2012).

Empirical research requires not only description but also explanation of translation phenomena. Why, for instance, are translated texts more explicit than originals? It has been suggested that explicitation as a feature of translated texts is a rather heterogeneous phenomenon and can be subdivided into four different types: the first three classes are linked to contrastive and cultural differences, whereas instances of the fourth type are specific to the translation process (Klaudy 1998: 82–83). Other researchers propose to explain translation phenomena in general through contrastive differences between ST and TT, register characteristics and a set of factors connected to the translation process, for instance those related to the process of understanding (Steiner 2001). Thus, studies using parallel corpora have shown that the majority of examples of explicitation found in the data can be accounted for through contrastive, register and/or cultural differences (Hansen-Schirra, Neumann & Steiner 2007; Becher 2010). Based on these corpus-based studies researchers can formulate hypotheses that ascribe the remaining instances to the characteristics of the translation process, and then test these hypotheses by considering data gathered during translation experiments, e.g. through keystroke logging. Keystroke logging software such as *Translog* (Jakobsen & Schou 1999) allows researchers to study intermediate steps of translations by recording all keystrokes and mouse clicks during the process of translation. Based on this behavioral data and the intermediate versions of translations, assumptions with regard to cognitive processing during translation can be made. Analysis of translation process data helps explain the properties of translation products, describe potential translation problems and identify translation strategies.

Previous studies in this area have focused on analysis of pauses and the number as well as length of the segments in between (e.g. Dragsted 2005; Jakobsen 2005; Alves & Vale 2009; 2011). Furthermore, translation styles have been investigated in both quantitative and qualitative manners (e.g. Pagano & Silva 2008; Carl, Dragsted & Jakobsen 2011), for example, the performances of professional and student translators have been compared with regard to speed of text production during translation, length of produced chunks and revision patterns (e.g. Jakobsen 2005).

In order to generalize beyond individual translation sessions and individual experiments, keystroke logging data has to be treated as a corpus (Alves & Magalhaes 2004; Alves & Vale 2009; 2011). In other words, the data has to be organized in such a way as to allow querying for specific recurring patterns (Carl & Jakobsen 2009) which can be analyzed both in terms of extra-linguistic factors such as age and gender of the translator, or time pressure, as well as linguistic features such as level of grammatical complexity, or word order. The latter research questions require additional linguistic annotation of the keystroke logging data (see §2.3). Thus, the aim of the present study is to create a keystroke logged corpus (KLC) and to perform linguistically informed quantitative analyses of the translation process data.

§2 describes the translation experiment data which serves as a prototype of a keystroke logged corpus, as well as the required pre-processing and linguistic annotation necessary for corpus queries, which are introduced in §3. A summary and a short outlook are provided in §4.[1]

2 Keystroke logged translation corpus

2.1 Data

The first prototype of the keystroke logged translation corpus is based on the translation process data collected in the framework of the project PROBRAL[2] in cooperation with the University of Saarland, Germany and the Federal University of Minas Gerais, Brazil. In the translation experiment participants were asked to translate a text from English into German (their L1). No time restrictions were imposed. The data from 16 participants is available: eight of them are professional translators with at least two years of experience and the other eight participants are PhD students of physics. Since the source text is an abridged version of an authentic text dealing with physics (see Appendix), the second group of participants are considered domain specialists. The original text was published in the popular-scientific magazine *Scientific American Online*, and the translation brief involved instructions to write a translation for another popular-scientific publication. The text was locally manipulated by integrating ten stimuli representing two different degrees of grammatical complexity, illustrated in (1) and (2). Based on previous research in Systemic Functional Linguistics (see Halliday &

---

[1] The project e-cosmos is funded by the Excellence Initiative of the German State and Federal Governments.
[2] The project was funded by CAPES–DAAD PROBRAL (292/2008).

Matthiessen 2014: 715; Taverniers 2003: 8–10), we assume that in the complex version the information is more dense and less explicit. For instance, whereas the italicized stretches of text in (1) and (2) contain the same semantic content, its realization as a clause in (1) leads to an explicit mention of the agents, namely the researchers, which are left out in the nominalized version presented in (2). During the experiment every participant translated one of the two versions of the text, in which simple and complex stimuli had been counterbalanced. In other words, five simple and five complex stimuli integrated into the first source text corresponded to the complex and simple variants of the same stimuli in the second text. The only translation resource allowed during the translation task was the online bilingual dictionary *leo*.[3] The participants' keystrokes, mouse movements and pauses in between were recorded using the software *Translog*. Additionally, the information on gaze points and pupil diameter was collected with the help of the remote eye-tracker *Tobii 2150*, using the corresponding software *Tobii Studio*, version 1.5 (Tobii Technology 2008). Currently the corpus considers only the keystroke logging data, but later the various data sources will be triangulated (see Alves 2003) to complement each other. The discussion of individual queries and specific examples in §3 indicates how the analysis of the data could benefit from the additional data stream.

(1) Simple stimulus
Instead of collapsing to a final fixed size, the height of the crushed ball continued to decrease, even three weeks *after the researchers had applied the weight.* (PROBRAL Source text 2)

(2) Complex stimulus
Instead of collapsing to a final fixed size, the height of the crushed ball continued to decrease, even three weeks *after the application of weight.* (PROBRAL Source text 1)

The prototype of the KLC thus consists of 2 versions of the original (source texts), 16 translations (target texts) as well as 16 log files (process texts). The source and target texts together amount to approximately 3,650 words, not including the process texts. The total size, taking into account various versions of the same target text words, can be determined only after completion of the pre-processing step (see §2.2). All the texts belong to the register of popular scientific writing. After the gold standard is established, the corpus will be extended to include data from further translation experiments, e.g. data stored in

---

[3] http://dict.leo.org/ende/index_de.html.

the CRITT TPR–DB (Carl 2012).[4] This database is a collection of keystroke logging and eye-tracking data recorded during translation, editing and post-editing experiments. It provides both raw and processed data: for instance, originals and final translation products are tokenized, aligned and annotated with parts of speech, whereas the process data is analyzed in terms of gaze and keystroke units (Carl 2012). According to the website, the current version of the database consists of approximately 1300 experiments.[5] In the development of our keystroke logged translation corpus we go further by identifying all potential tokens produced during a translation process and enriching these with linguistic information. At the moment, the relatively small size of the corpus is sufficient to develop the new procedures and queries required for this type of data.

2.2 Pre-processing

While the originals and the final translations can be automatically annotated and aligned using existing tools, the process texts require pre-processing before they can be enriched with further information. The keystroke logs consist of individual events corresponding to one press of a key or a mouse. To link this behavioral information to the linguistic level of analysis, the events have to be represented in terms of complete tokens. Since the intentions of a translator are not always clear, it is essential to reflect all possible tokens produced during the translation process. Using a modified version of the concept of target hypotheses that Lüdeling (2008) introduced for learner corpora (which also contain non-standard language with errors), the KLC will include multiple layers of annotation reflecting different versions of the same tokens that could be inferred from the process data. Thus, in our context, target hypotheses represent potential translation plans. Several hypotheses are annotated when the keystroke logging data is ambiguous, i.e. in cases when, based on the pressed keys, it is unclear what token the translator intended to produce, and when the process contains additional indicators of increased cognitive processing such as longer pauses or corrections. This method retains the necessary level of objectivity because it does not force the researcher to select only the version which appears most plausible at a certain stage of corpus compilation.

Leijten et al. (2012) discuss the processing of monolingual keystroke logging data by aggregating it from the character (keystroke) to the word level (see also

---

[4] The CRITT TPR–DB is the Translation Process Research Database of the Centre for Research and Innovation in Translation and Translation Technology.

[5] https://sites.google.com/site/centretranslationinnovation .

Macken et al. 2012). For translation data, however, the required processing is more complex. Within the target text keystrokes are aligned to tokens, and these tokens (representing intermediate versions of words either preserved in the TT, or modified/deleted in the process) are in turn aligned to the alignment units consisting of ST–TT counterparts (see Carl 2009: 227). The same process of alignment is also performed for the phrase and grammatical function levels. These alignment links make it possible to query for all intermediate versions of individual tokens and phrases (see §3.5).

To facilitate this alignment, an alignment tool was developed which allows the researcher to manually select items to be aligned from the ST and the TT.[6] These alignment units are saved in the same keystroke logging file. The screenshot in Figure 1 shows the selection of an alignment pair with the tool: the words *explaining* from the ST list and *erklären* 'to explain' from the TT list are highlighted to become alignment pair 0 in the bottom window. The window on the left part of the screen displays the XML file for reference.

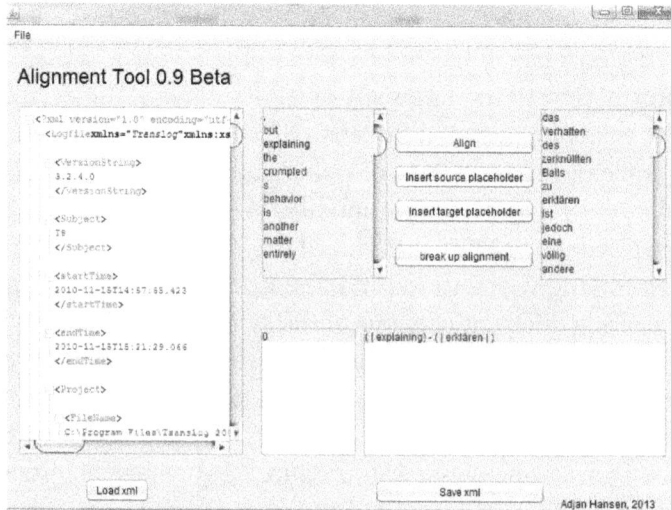

Figure 1: Screenshot of an alignment process using the alignment tool

The *Translog* software supplies the keystroke data in XML format. Each keystroke is identified as a log event containing values for the type of action (i.e., character, deletion, movement, mouse click), the cursor position of this keystroke, a time stamp and a block ID which identifies the number of characters

---

[6] The tool was developed by students Adjan Hansen-Ampah (RWTH Aachen) and Chuan Yao (Georgia Institute of Technology) during a UROP project at RWTH Aachen University in 2013.

highlighted in the log event (e.g. when a segment is highlighted prior to being moved or deleted). During the pre-processing stage for the prototype, the XML data was enriched by aggregating the log events into plausible tokens to which token IDs were assigned. For each alignment level (currently only word level; in the future also phrase and grammatical function levels) a reference link was specified to link the object to the corresponding alignment unit created by the aligner. If the token did not appear in the final version and could not be linked to any existing alignment units, the reference link was designated as an empty link. In example (3) below the three words *für Verwirrung sorgt* 'causes confusion', which appear in an intermediate version of this sentence, are characterized by empty links: since the same semantic information is expressed in the final version through a different grammatical structure using non-related lexical items, namely *nicht vollständig erklären können* 'could not explain entirely', the tokens cannot be connected to any alignment units. The reference to the empty links ensures that the information contained in the intermediate versions is preserved in the data and can be queried. These tokens can only be linked on the level of units larger than words. The frequent use of semantically equivalent structures rather than structurally similar units requires alignment on multiple levels, as certain relations cannot be captured at the level of individual words.[7]

(3)   EO: Yet it displays surprising strength and resists further
        compression, *a fact that has confounded physicists.* (PROBRAL)

   GT_i: ♦★★ eine♦ Tatsache,♦ die♦
                   a   fact   the

   Physikerf♦★ ⊲⊠⊲⊠♦[★11.968]⊲⊠ ⊲⊠ ⊲⊠ ⊲⊠ ⊲⊠ ⊲⊠ ⊲⊠ ⊲⊠
   physicists

   bei♦ Physikern♦ für♦ Verwirrung♦ sorgrt⊲⊠ ⊲⊠t.
   by   physicists   for   confusion   caters

   GT_f eine Tatsache, die sich   Physiker noch immer nicht
            a   fact   that themselves physicists yet   still   not
   vollständig erklären können
   entirely   explain can

---

[7] The intermediate versions of German translations use special characters introduced in linear representation, a visualization option provided by the keystroke logging software *Translog*. ♦ – a space character, ★ – approx. 1 sec. pause, [★36.721] – a pause of 36 seconds, 721 milliseconds, ⊲⊠ – a backspace character. The part of the original corresponding to the translation is written in italics. One or more intermediate versions (GT_i) and the final version (GT_f) of translations, if relevant for the discussion, are presented in their chronological order.

Similarly, empty links were also defined in the ST–TT alignment units, if no corresponding element could be identified for either the ST or the TT (Čulo et al. 2012), so that this information can also be extracted from the corpus.

2.3 Annotation

"Corpus annotation adds value to a corpus in that it considerably extends the range of research questions that a corpus can readily address" (McEnery, Xiao & Tono 2006: 29): a systematic annotation of particular information types throughout a corpus enables researchers to search for and extract corpus examples based on certain criteria included in one or more annotation layers. At the moment all texts are annotated with meta-information specifying the participant ID, a version of the translated text and the participant's group (translator/physicist). The meta-information will be extended to include further variables relevant for potential analyses of the translation process data, e.g. participant-specific metadata such as age or native language (see Hvelplund & Carl 2012). Furthermore, the KLC will contain several layers of linguistic annotation. The part of speech (POS) annotation of the process texts was done manually for some examples in the corpus prototype, but the aim is to perform this step automatically for process as well as source and target texts through the use of an existing tagger. Automatic syntactic parsing and annotation of grammatical functions is also planned;[8] however, it is recognized that manual interaction to check the results will still be necessary. The multilayer annotation (see Hansen-Schirra, Neumann & Vela 2006) will be extended by integrating the target hypotheses as a separate annotation layer (see §3.2). In addition, behavioral information such as the length of individual pauses (see Alves & Vale 2009; 2011) will be annotated to facilitate quantifying these types of features, as well as querying for a combination of behavioral and linguistic information.

3 Possible queries

Depending on the research questions, different types of queries into the translation process data are required. The following sub-sections describe a selection of possible queries. Taking into account the novelty of this corpus type for transla-

---

[8] Different taggers and parsers will be tested, and in a later step trained to accommodate the non-standard features present in the KLC. The ongoing work on pre-processing and annotation of monolingual process data (Leijten et al. 2012; Macken et al. 2012) is being taken into consideration.

tion process research, this section aims at showing the potential applications of the planned annotation and alignment layers introduced above for the analysis of translations.

3.1 Alternative versions and incomplete structures within individual intermediate versions

One query type concerns alternative versions of an unfolding target text. During the process of translation, evolving texts typically undergo multiple revisions (e.g. in the form of deletions, overwrites or additions) before the final product is completed. One way of looking at revisions is to consider all keystrokes related to the translation of one source text sentence, up to the point where the translator begins translating other sentences, as an intermediate version of the translation of this source text sentence. The next version is identified, when and if the translation of this sentence is resumed after text production and/or revision of other passages.[9] Often such intermediate versions could function on their own: their linguistic structures are complete and could be left unchanged throughout the translation session. However, for various reasons, subsequent revisions may lead to (a series of) changes in these structures, thus creating new versions of the same sentences.

A single intermediate version may include several alternatives for the same linguistic slot realized by the same part of speech. For example, in (4), two versions of the modal verb within a subordinate clause have been supplied by the translator: the first of these in the present (*können* 'can') and the second in the past tense (*konnten* 'could'), separated by a slash.

(4)   **EO:** *Yet it displays surprising strength and resists* further compression, a fact that has confounded physicists. (PROBRAL)

GT_i: [...] die◆   sich◆   Physiker◆ nicht◆ erklären◆
             which themselves physicists not   explain
können☆/konnten.
can/could

The part of speech annotation allows us to query this and similar patterns through a search for identical parts of speech separated by a punctuation mark. Figure 2 shows the XML code provided by the keystroke logging software *Translog*

---

[9] The identification of intermediate versions differs from the annotation of different target hypotheses (see §3.2): for instance, in (4), one intermediate version corresponds to two target hypotheses.

```
<t id="38" token="können" xlink:href="tAlign#28" xlink:href="emptylink
    #5">
    <LogEvent Action="1" Value="107" Cursor="477" Block="0" Time="00
        :04:59:694" />
    <LogEvent Action="1" Value="246" Cursor="478" Block="0" Time="00
        :04:59:850" />
    <LogEvent Action="1" Value="110" Cursor="479" Block="0" Time="00
        :05:00:294" />
    <LogEvent Action="1" Value="110" Cursor="480" Block="0" Time="00
        :05:00:447" />
    <LogEvent Action="1" Value="101" Cursor="481" Block="0" Time="00
        :05:00:559" />
    <LogEvent Action="1" Value="110" Cursor="482" Block="0" Time="00
        :05:00:672" />
    </t>
<t id="39" token="/" xlink:href="emptylink#6">
    <LogEvent Action="1" Value="47" Cursor="483" Block="0" Time="00
        :05:01:938" />
    </t>
<t id="40" token="konnten" xlink:href="tAlign#28" xlink:href="emptylink
    #7">
    <LogEvent Action="1" Value="107" Cursor="484" Block="0" Time="00
        :05:02:346" />
    <LogEvent Action="1" Value="111" Cursor="485" Block="0" Time="00
        :05:02:498" />
    <LogEvent Action="1" Value="110" Cursor="486" Block="0" Time="00
        :05:02:682" />
    <LogEvent Action="1" Value="110" Cursor="487" Block="0" Time="00
        :05:02:809" />
    <LogEvent Action="1" Value="116" Cursor="488" Block="0" Time="00
        :05:02:961" />
    <LogEvent Action="1" Value="101" Cursor="489" Block="0" Time="00
        :05:03:041" />
    <LogEvent Action="1" Value="110" Cursor="490" Block="0" Time="00
        :05:03:121" />
    </t>
```

Figure 2: XML code enriched with alignment links and information on tokens and
parts of speech

corresponding to the production of the tokens *können* and *konnten* in example
(4). As can be seen, the tool generates files representing one log event (e.g. a
keystroke corresponding to a letter or a slash) per line. The pre-processing step
requires the grouping of these events into tokens, such as *können* and *konnten*,
which can be then annotated with part of speech tags. Here we use the tags
from the Stuttgart-Tübingen Tagset (STTS) for German (Schiller et al. 1999) for
the purposes of illustration. Both *können* 'can' in Token 38 and *konnten* 'could'
in Token 40 bear the part of speech tag VMFIN indicating 'verb finite, modal'.

Sometimes, alternatives might fill not only one part of speech slot but a whole phrase or clause, requiring a different approach in order to query for such more complex intermediate versions. The present study differentiates between words occurring in the ST and the TT, on the one hand, and different tokens that can be identified in the intermediate versions. From the perspective of the process all meaningful items in the intermediate versions are tokens. In addition, those tokens that are kept in the final translation are designated as words. This distinction helps us keep the process and the product of translation apart and study their interrelations. For instance, combinations between one or several words and a larger number of tokens, present in the same intermediate translation version, are considered to be an indicator that several alternatives for the same linguistic unit are included. Querying for such combinations would result in a more complete list of examples similar to (4).

However, in some cases a translator leaves a stretch of text unfinished by either writing less or more linguistic material than is required for a complete linguistic structure. Rather than adding multiple alternatives to a single translation version, a translator may also write an incomplete structure, in which a placeholder is substituted for the later linguistic unit, such as a sequence of characters "xxx" or simply several space characters, as is shown in (5). In this sequence of word classes ART ADJA * KON VVFIN (article adjective * coordinating conjunction finite verb), the head noun of the noun phrase is missing. For this reason, searches for such examples also require POS annotation of the intermediate versions.

(5)   **EO:** *Yet it displays surprising strength and resists* further compression, a fact that has confounded physicists. (PROBRAL)

GT_i: Denno★ch◆★★★★★★ zeigt★◆ sie◆ eine◆
      yet   displays it   a
      Er◁☒◁☒◁☒◆erstaun★★liche◆ [★36.721] ◆◆★
      suprising◆◆◆   ◆◆
      und◆★★★★★★★ widersteht[…].
      and   resists

Examples of the phenomena described in this sub-section can be seen as indications of understanding difficulties or attempts at finding the most suitable translation of the ST unit. The translator is aware of the problems and, rather than taking the time to optimize this section at that point, s/he prefers to continue translating the text, intending to return to this passage later. These examples can be investigated in terms of the translation strategies that are employed by translators. It is possible that the strategies differ not simply from translator to translator, but also depending on linguistic factors such as the grammatical complexity of the original.

3.2 Alternative target hypotheses

As mentioned earlier, some tokens found in the intermediate versions may be ambiguous: in these cases, the researcher cannot determine the intention of the translator. Here it is essential not to interpret the data but rather reflect all possible options by annotating several target hypotheses (Lüdeling 2008). In example (6) below, the preposition *innerhalb* and the indefinite article *eines* are followed by a longer pause, after which the ending of the article is changed, turning *eines* into *einer*. Since articles in German contain morphological endings expressing the grammatical categories of person, number, gender and case, one different letter can affect the grammatical structure of the noun phrase. The researcher can, therefore, formulate a target hypothesis that the original plan for the noun phrase was *eines Zylinders* 'a$_{\text{GEN.M}}$ cylinder', where the masculine genitive form of the determiner (matching the masculine noun) was typed, after which the translation plan changed. As a result, the translator deleted the –*s* at the end of *eines*, typed the –*r* instead (yielding the feminine form of the determiner *einer*) and continued typing to produce the feminine noun *Zylindergeometrie* 'a$_{\text{GEN.F}}$ cylinder geometry'. Although only the token *Zylindergeometrie* is evident at this point in the translation process, the existence of the assumed first version is supported by the fact that, at a later stage of the translation process, *Zylindergeometrie* was altered to *Zylinder*. It is plausible that the text-editing operations leading to a different grammatical suffix – especially if preceded by a longer pause (a potential indicator of increased cognitive processing, see Dragsted 2005) – do not represent the correction of a simple typing error, but rather reflect a more complex cognitive process of changes to the translation plan. Still, the researcher cannot discount the possibility that the change from –*s* to –*r* is in fact a simple correction of a typo. This scenario constitutes another target hypothesis.

(6)   **EO:** The researchers crumpled a sheet of thin aluminized Mylar and then placed it *inside a cylinder* equipped with a piston to crush the sheet. (PROBRAL)

   GT_i: [...] innerhalb♦ eines★♦★★★★★◁⊠⟨⊠r♦
            inside   a$_{\text{GEN.M}}$★♦★★★★★a$_{\text{GEN.F}}$
            Z★ylindergeometrie [...].
            cylinder.geometry$_{\text{GEN.F.}}$

Planned annotation of alternative target hypotheses will allow querying for such patterns.[10] These can be analyzed with regard to more or less technical vocabulary, as is the case in example (6) above, verbal or nominal variants, etc. Taking into account a number of explanatory factors, such as register characteristics or process-related variables, a comprehensive picture on such alternations will emerge.

3.3 Incorrect combinations of morphological markings in the final product

Analyzing the final product in terms of its quality, the researcher may come across grammatical errors, as in (7).

(7)   **EO:** *The researchers crumpled a sheet of thin aluminized Mylar.*
        (PROBRAL)

    GT_i: *Die Wissenschaftler zerknitterten eine dünne Alufolie*
        the scientists   crumpled   a   thin   aluminium.foil

    GT_f: *Die Wissenschaftler zerknitterten eine dünnes Blatt*
        the scientists   crumpled   a   thin   sheet
        Alufolie
        aluminium.foil

The grammatical rule in German requires that in noun phrases, not only articles and nouns but also premodifying adjectives agree in person, number, gender and case. For instance, in (7) the intermediate version contains the noun phrase *eine dünne Alufolie* 'a thin aluminium foil'. The head noun *Alufolie* 'aluminium foil' has the following characteristics: third person singular, feminine gender and accusative case. Therefore, the indefinite article *ein* 'a' and the adjective *dünn* 'thin' are used with the ending *-e* indicating the same person, number, gender and case. In the final version the corresponding NP has the form *eine dünnes Blatt Alufolie* 'a thin sheet of aluminium foil': here the head noun is no longer *Alufolie* 'aluminium foil' but rather the noun *Blatt* 'sheet', having the same person, number and case but different gender, namely neuter. To agree with the head noun along these four paramaters, the ending of the adjective has been changed to *-es* and the article should have been modified into *ein* 'a_ACC.N'. However, this rule has not been observed.

---

[10] Since the notion of target hypotheses was originally developed for annotation of learner corpora, it has to be modified to be compatible with the translation process data.

Considering not only the source and the target texts but also intermediate versions of translation helps understand how the grammatical error has been introduced into the final product: the noun phrase *a sheet of thin aluminized Mylar* was initially translated to the noun *Alufolie* 'aluminium foil' and then changed during a (later) revision phase into *Blatt Alufolie* 'sheet of aluminium foil', which is more similar to the original than the first attempt. The level of explicitness of the ST is recreated by specifying that exactly one sheet of the foil rather than simply aluminium foil was crumpled. During this revision the morphological ending of the preceding adjective was changed to agree in gender with the new head noun *Blatt* 'sheet', but the ending of the article was not modified accordingly. Since all translations were performed into the native language of test subjects, grammatical inconsistencies are not necessarily due to a lack of grammatical competence. One possible explanation could be that the increased cognitive effort during translation of this noun phrase led to a grammatical error in the final version, possibly by drawing the cognitive resources away from the grammatical article. This hypothesis can be further tested by triangulating the keystroke logging data to such eye-tracking variables as number and length of fixations or pupil dilation, which are typically used in the eye-tracking research to operationalize cognitive demands (e.g. Pavlović & Hvelplund 2009).

3.4 Substitutions of word classes

Translation studies research has a long tradition of studying the phenomenon of translation shifts, i.e. various changes introduced during the translation process and visible in the translation product. A parallel corpus of aligned originals and translations allows a systematic analysis of shifts between translation units of various sizes and on different level of linguistic analysis. For instance, a recent corpus-based study has concentrated on shifts between different word classes (Čulo et al. 2008), the so-called "transpositions" (Vinay & Darbelnet 1995: 36). Example (8) illustrates a change from the verb *require* in the English original to the adjective *erforderlich* 'necessary' in the final version of the German translation.

(8)   **EO:** *Crumpling a sheet of paper seems simple and doesn't require much effort* (PROBRAL)

        GT_i: *Ein Blatt Papier zu zerknüllen, scheint eine einfache Sache zu*
            a   sheet paper to crumple   seems a   simple thing to
           sein und benötigt nicht viel   Kraftaufwand.
           be and requires not   much effort

GT_f: *Ein Blatt Papier zu zerknüllen, scheint eine einfache Sache zu*
      a   sheet paper to crumple   seems   a   simple   thing to
      sein, und scheinbar ist dazu   auch nicht viel   Kraftaufwand
      be   and apparently is for.that also not   much effort
      erforderlich
      necessary

It is possible to extract this translation shift from a verb in the ST to an adjective in the TT using an available English-German parallel corpus such as CroCo (Hansen-Schirra & Steiner 2012). However, this kind of product-oriented corpus does not contain the information on what happened to the original verb in the intermediate translation versions. As is shown in (8), the translation shift was not introduced until a later revision of the pattern: the verb *benötigen* 'require', initially used as a translation of the English verb, was replaced at a later stage by an adjective integrated into a different clause-level structure. The opposite pattern is also possible, in which a translation shift present in the intermediate version disappears during further editing of the translation. Thus, a keystroke logged corpus enables researchers to extract shifts present at different stages of the translation development and to compare, for instance, the two possible revision patterns involving changes of word classes.

Previous studies have suggested that translation involves a process of understanding during which the semantic content of the ST has to be unpacked by the translator. In other words, it is assumed that certain highly dense grammatical structures are typically understood in terms of grammatically less complex patterns. A number of factors influencing translations, such as contrastive differences, register characteristics or other translation process-dependent variables (e.g. time pressure), might lead to changes with respect to the level of grammatical complexity of the corresponding TT unit, depending on how information is repacked by the translator (Steiner 2001; Hansen-Schirra & Steiner 2012). Shifts of grammatical complexity have been operationalized as shifts of word classes. Thus, for example, the same semantic information can be expressed either as a clause or as a noun phrase; in the latter case the described event is presented in a more compressed manner, making certain aspects implicit. By looking at shifts between verbs and nouns, such changes of complexity can be analyzed further. The addition of intermediate versions allows the investigation of how often and under which circumstances the level of grammatical complexity is changed during the process of translation.

(9)   **EO:** *Once a paper ball is scrunched, it is more than 75 percent air.*
(PROBRAL)

GT_i: *nachdem der Papierball zusammengedrückt wurde besteht er*
after   the paper.ball together.pressed   was   consists it
zu mehr als 75 Prozent aus Luft.
to more that 75 percent of   air

GT_f: *Ein zusammengedrückter Papierball besteht zu mehr als   75*
a   together.pressed   paper.ball consists to more than 75
Prozent aus Luft
percent of   air

In (9), the professional translator has initially kept the structure of the original sentence: a temporal adverbial expressed through a subordinate clause is present in both the ST and the intermediate version of the TT. However, during the final revision the clause was turned into an NP by using a strategy of premodification typical for German, namely a reduced participle clause. This compression of semantic information results in a more complex grammatical structure in the German translation than in the English original. It has been suggested that one of the factors leading to the increase of grammatical complexity could be high translation competence (Hansen-Schirra & Steiner 2012: 260). To test this hypothesis, the frequency of similar examples in translations by professional translators and physicists could be compared and submitted to statistical tests.

3.5 Lexical substitutions

As mentioned in §2.2, the alignment units defined between corresponding words, phrases or chunks in the ST and the TT function as reference points to which the process tokens are linked during the pre-processing of the data. Using these reference links a researcher can trace the history of the TT word. While the previous section discussed an example in which a verb in the intermediate version is linked to an adjective in the final TT, a revision does not necessarily affect the grammatical structure of a sentence. Thus, as is shown in example (10), the changes could also be at a lower level of complexity: in this sentence only the noun slot is repeatedly modified before the translator found the solution that s/he considered to be most suitable. This and similar instances found in the KLC are interpreted in terms of register characteristics or stylistic reasons (e.g. avoidance of repetitions).

(10)   **EO:**   *is another matter entirely* (PROBRAL)

    GT_i1: *so ist dies eine völlig andere   Sache*
          so is this a   totally different thing

    GT_i2: *so ist dies eine völlig andere   Angelegenheit*
          so is this a   totally different matter

    GT_f: *so ist dies eine völlig andere   Frage*
          so is this a   totally different question

This particular example illustrates that the alignment of process tokens involves a certain level of interpretation on the part of the researcher: according to Kollberg & Severinson-Eklundh (2001: 92), "if a writer deletes a word, and subsequently inserts another word at the same position in the text, one cannot deduce that the writer intended the second word to replace the first (even if this is often the case)". In other words, the authors indicate that though it might seem obvious to assume that the writer/translator meant to substitute a certain word, this is still an interpretation by the researcher and, therefore, does not belong to the formal level of data description. The functional analysis should be left to a later research stage (Kollberg & Severinson-Eklundh 2001: 92–93). The distinction between formal and functional data pre-processing can be compared to formal and functional types of annotation found in the corpora. For instance, on the formal level, sentences can be parsed into individual phrases, whereas an additional functional annotation would involve enrichment of these units with grammatical functions. The present study takes the position that both types of pre-processing and annotation are required. This combination of formal and functional levels facilitates different types of analyses. Thus, it is possible to analyze the data in a more qualitative manner by looking at individual sentences or texts; in this case the formal pre-processing of the keystroke logging data might be enough. At the same time, the queries discussed in this article are designed to conduct quantitative investigations, which certainly benefit from additional functional types of pre-processing and annotation. As long as all of the decisions involved in these processes are made transparent, the researcher can assess which information stored in the corpus is required for each individual case.

4 Conclusion and outlook

In this paper we have described the compilation and annotation of a keystroke logged corpus containing original and translated texts along with the process texts, with the aim of tracing the development of the linguistic phenomena found in the final product through the intermediate versions of the unfolding text during the translation process. This requires complex alignment procedures on several levels of analysis together with multilayer annotation to include information such as target hypotheses and typical translation features (e.g. grammatical shifts). The corpus will allow us to query the data in order to discover consistencies or compare intermediate versions, and to understand more about the translation process; thus, while it is particularly the quantitative research into the translation process that will be facilitated through this type of corpus, the interpretation of these quantitative findings requires taking a more qualitative perspective on the data.

The next steps in the development of the corpus are undertaken within the work of the RWTH Boost Fund project *e-cosmos*. The goal of *e-cosmos* is to develop a transparent and user-friendly environment for the quantitative analysis of complex, multimodal humanities data, and at the same time allow researchers to interact with the data, from the collection stage through (semi-automatic) annotation to the application of a wide range of statistical tests. This approach has two immediate consequences for the translation data: 1) the data outputs and formats generated by the parsers and other tools selected for work with the data will be compatible; and 2) the platform will enable the analysis of the keystroke data together with other data streams such as the eye-tracking data, thereby allowing more fine-grained quantitative analyses. The combined analysis of the data on translation process and product will contribute to a comprehensive understanding of the various factors playing a role in translation.

Appendix

Shortened original

Crumpling a sheet of paper seems simple enough and certainly doesn't require much effort, but explaining why the resulting crinkled ball behaves the way it does is another matter entirely. Once scrunched, a paper ball is more than 75 percent air yet displays surprising strength and resists further compression, a fact that has confounded physicists. A report in the February 18 issue of *Physical Review Letters*, though, describes one aspect of the behavior of crumpled sheets: how their size changes in relation to the force they withstand.

A crushed thin sheet is essentially a mass of conical points connected by curved ridges, which store energy. When the sheet is further compressed, these ridges collapse and smaller ones form, increasing the amount of stored energy within the wad. Sidney Nagel and colleagues of the University of Chicago modeled how the force required to compress the ball relates to its size. After crumpling a sheet of thin aluminized Mylar, the researchers placed it inside a cylinder equipped with a piston to crush the crumpled sheet. Instead of collapsing to a final fixed size as expected, the team writes, the height of the crushed ball continued to decrease, even three weeks after the weight was applied [...].

Graham, Sarah. 2002. A New Report Explains the Physics of Crumpled Paper *Scientific American Online.* http://www.scientificamerican.com/article.cfm?id=a-new-report-explains-the.

Source text 1

Crumpling a sheet of paper seems simple and doesn't require much effort, but ex-plaining *why the crumpled ball behaves the way it does* is another matter entirely. *A scrunched paper ball* is more than 75 percent air. Yet it displays surprising strength and *resistance to further compression,* a fact that has confounded physi-cists. A report in Physical Review Letters, though, describes one aspect of the behavior of crumpled sheets: *how their size changes* in relation to the force they withstand. A crushed thin sheet is essentially a mass of conical points connected by *curved energy-storing ridges. When the sheet is further compressed,* these ridges collapse and smaller ones form, increasing the amount of stored energy within the wad. Scientists at the University of Chicago modeled *how the force required to compress the ball relates to its size. After the crumpling of a sheet of thin aluminized Mylar,* the researchers placed it inside a cylinder. *They equipped the cylinder with a piston* to crush the sheet. Instead of collapsing to a final fixed size, the height of the crushed ball continued to decrease, even three weeks *after the application of weight.*

Source text 2

Crumpling a sheet of paper seems simple and doesn't require much effort, but explaining *the crumpled ball's behavior* is another matter entirely. *Once a paper ball is scrunched,* it is more than 75 percent air. Yet it displays surprising strength and *resists further compression,* a fact that has confounded physicists. A report in Physical Review Letters, though, describes one aspect of the behavior of crum-pled sheets: *changes in their size* in relation to the force they withstand.

A crushed thin sheet is essentially a mass of conical points connected by *curved ridges, which store energy. In the event of further compression of the sheet* these ridges collapse and smaller ones form, increasing the amount of stored energy within the wad. Scientists at the University of Chicago modeled *the relation be-tween compression force and ball size. The researchers crumpled a sheet of thin alu-minized Mylar and then* placed it inside *a cylinder equipped with a piston* to crush the sheet. Instead of collapsing to a final fixed size, the height of the crushed ball continued to decrease, even three weeks *after the researchers had applied the weight.*

References

Alves, Fabio (ed.). 2003. *Triangulating translation: Perspectives in process oriented research.* Amsterdam: John Benjamins.

Alves, Fabio & Célia Magalhaes. 2004. Using small corpora to tap and map the process-product interface in translation. *TradTerm* 10. 179–211.

Alves, Fabio & Daniel Couto Vale. 2009. Probing the unit of translation in time: Aspects of the design and development of a web application for storing, anno-tating, and querying translation process data. *Across Languages and Cultures* 10(2). 251–273.

Alves, Fabio & Daniel Couto Vale. 2011. On drafting and revision in translation: A corpus linguistics oriented analysis of translation process data. *Translation: Computation, Corpora, Cognition* 1. 105–122.

Baker, Mona. 1996. Corpus-based translation studies: The challenges that lie ahead. In Harold Somers (ed.), *Terminology, LSP and translation: Studies in language engineering in honour of Juan C. Sager*, 175–186. Amsterdam: John Benjamins.

Becher, Viktor. 2010. Abandoning the notion of "translation-inherent" explicita-tion: Against a dogma of translation studies. *Across Languages and Cultures* 11(1). 1–28.

Carl, Michael. 2009. Triangulating product and process data: Quantifying align-ment units with keystroke data. *Copenhagen Studies in Language* 38. 225–247.

Carl, Michael. 2012. The CRITT TPR-DB 1.0: A database for empirical human translation process research. In Sharon O'Brien, Michel Simard & Lucia Specia (eds.), *Proceedings of the AMTA 2012 workshop on post-editing technology and practice (WPTP 2012)*, 9–18. Stroudsburg: Association for Machine Translation in the Americas (AMTA).

Carl, Michael, Barbara Dragsted & Arnt Lykke Jakobsen. 2011. A taxonomy of human translation styles. *Translation Journal* 16(2). http://translationjournal. net/journal/56taxonomy.htm.

Carl, Michael & Arnt Lykke Jakobsen. 2009. Objectives for a query language for user-activity data. In *In 6th international natural language processing and cognitive science workshop.* Milano.

Dragsted, Barbara. 2005. Segmentation in translation: Differences across levels of expertise and difficulty. *Target* 17(1). 49–70.

Göpferich, Susanne. 2008. *Translationsprozessforschung: Stand - Methoden - Perspektiven.* Tübingen: Narr.

Halliday, Michael Alexander Kirkwood & Christian Matthiessen. 2014. *Halliday's introduction to functional grammar.* 4th edition. London: Routledge.

Hansen-Schirra, Silvia, Stella Neumann & Erich Steiner. 2007. Cohesive explicitness and explicitation in an English-German translation corpus. *Languages in contrast: International journal for contrastive linguistics* 7(2). 241–265.

Hansen-Schirra, Silvia, Stella Neumann & Michaela Vela. 2006. Multi-dimensional annotation and alignment in an English-German translation corpus. In *In proceedings of the 5th workshop on NLP and XML (NLPXML-2006): Multi-dimensional markup in Natural Language Processing*, 35–42. Trento: EACL.

Hansen-Schirra, Silvia & Erich Steiner. 2012. Towards a typology of translation properties. In Silvia Hansen-Schirra, Stella Neumann & Erich Steiner (eds.), *Cross-linguistic corpora for the study of translations: Insights from the language pair English-German*, 255–280. Berlin: de Gruyter.

Hvelplund, Kristian Tangsgaard & Michael Carl. 2012. User activity metadata for reading, writing and translation research. In Victoria Arranz, Daan Broeder, Bertrand Gaiffe, Maria Gavrilidou, Monica Monachini & Thorsten Trippel (eds.), *Proceedings of the eighth international conference on language resources and evaluation*, 55–59. Paris: ELRA.

Jakobsen, Arnt Lykke. 2005. Instances of peak performance in translation. *Lebende Sprachen* 3. 111–116.

Jakobsen, Arnt Lykke & Lasse Schou. 1999. Translog documentation. In Gyde Hansen (ed.), *Probing the process in translation: Methods and results*, 9–20. Frederiksberg: Samfunds Litteratur.

Klaudy, Kinga. 1998. Explicitation. In Mona Baker (ed.), *Routledge encyclopedia of translation studies*, 80–84. London: Routledge.

Kollberg, Py & Kerstin Severinson-Eklundh. 2001. Studying writers' revising patterns with S-notation analysis. In Thierry Olive & Michael Levy (eds.), *Contemporary tools and techniques for studying writing*, 89–93. Kluwer Academic Publishers.

Laviosa, Sara. 2002. *Corpus-based translation studies: Theory, findings, applications.* Amsterdam: Rodopi.

Leijten, Mariëlle, Lieve Macken, Veronique Hoste, Eric Van Horenbeeck & Luuk Van Waes. 2012. From character to word level: Enabling the linguistic analyses of Inputlog process data. In *Proceedings of the second workshop on computational linguistics and writing*, 1–8. Avignon: Association for Computational Linguistics.

Lüdeling, Anke. 2008. Mehrdeutigkeiten und Kategorisierung: Probleme bei der Annotation von Lernerkorpora. In Maik Walter & Patrick Grommes (eds.), *Fortgeschrittene Lernervarietäten*, 119–140. Tübingen: Niemeyer.

Macken, Lieve, Veronique Hoste, Mariëlle Leijten & Luuk Van Waes. 2012. From keystrokes to annotated process data: Enriching the output of Inputlog with linguistic information. In *Proceedings of the international conference on language resources and evaluation*, 2224–2229. Paris: ELRA.

McEnery, Tony, Richard Xiao & Yukio Tono. 2006. *Corpus-based language studies: An advanced resource book*. London: Routledge.

Pagano, Adriana & Igor Silva. 2008. *Domain knowledge in translation task execution: Insights from academic researchers performing as translators*. Shanghai: XVIII FIT World Congress.

Pavlović, Natasa & Kristian Tangsgaard Hvelplund. 2009. Eye tracking translation directionality. In Anthony Pym & Alexander Perekrestenko (eds.), *Translation research projects 2*, 93–109. Tarragona: Intercultural Studies Group.

Schiller, Anne, Simone Teufel, Christine Stöckert & Christine Thielen. 1999. *Guidelines für das Tagging Deutscher Textcorpora mit STTS*. Universität Stuttgart, Universität Tübingen.

Steiner, Erich. 2001. Translations English-German: Investigating the relative importance of systemic contrasts and of the text type 'translation'. *SPRIKreports* 7. 1–49.

Taverniers, Miriam. 2003. Grammatical metaphor in SFL: A historiography of the introduction and initial study of the concept. In Anne-Marie Simon-Vandenbergen, Miriam Taverniers & Louise Ravelli (eds.), *Grammatical metaphor: Views from systemic functional linguistics*, 5–33. Amsterdam: John Benjamins.

Teich, Elke. 2003. *Cross-linguistic variation in system and text: A methodology for the investigation of translations and comparable texts*. Berlin: de Gruyter.

Tobii Technology. 2008. *Tobii Studio 1.X user manual*. http://www.tobii.com/Global/Analysis/Downloads/User_Manuals_and_Guides/Tobii_Studio1.X_UserManual.pdf.

Vinay, Jean-Paul & Jean Darbelnet. 1995. *Comparative stylistics of French and English: A methodology for translation*. Amsterdam: John Benjamins.

Čulo, Oliver, Silvia Hansen-Schirra, Stella Neumann & Mihaela Vela. 2008. Empirical studies on language contrast using the English-German comparable and parallel CroCo Corpus. In *Proceedings of the sixth international conference on language resources and evaluation*, 47–51. Paris: ELRA.

Čulo, Oliver, Silvia Hansen-Schirra, Karin Maksymski & Stella Neumann. 2012. Heuristic examination of translation shifts. In Silvia Hansen-Schirra, Stella Neumann & Erich Steiner (eds.), *Cross-linguistic corpora for the study of translations: Insights from the language pair English-German*, 255–280. Berlin: de Gruyter.

Chapter 3

Racism goes to the movies: A corpus-driven study of cross-linguistic racist discourse annotation and translation analysis

Effie Mouka, Ioannis E. Saridakis and Angeliki Fotopoulou

This paper traces register shifts (Halliday & Hasan 1976: 22; Hatim & Mason 1997) between source-texts (English) and target-texts (Greek and Spanish) in instances of racist discourse in films. It presents preliminary, as yet non-exhaustive, findings and aims to ultimately formulate explanatory hypotheses concerning the emerging norms. Our methodological approach is placed in the framework of Descriptive Translation Studies (Toury 2012; Chesterman 2008) and in the school of Critical Discourse Analysis (Fairclough 1985; 1992), relying on Appraisal Theory (Martin & White 2005) to provide and analyse a taxonomy of the racism-related utterances examined.

1 Introduction

Technological advances in Corpus Linguistics and tools for processing and compiling linguistic corpora open new ways on how we exploit textual and research material. In a descriptive approach, textual and pragmatic annotation can largely facilitate the systematic lexico-grammatical analysis of linguistic resources (see McEnery & Hardie 2012: 29–31; Zanettin 2012: 76–79). This holds true also for translation corpora, with a particular focus on the descriptive examination of translation strategies and norms (Zanettin 2012: 78–96).

Effie Mouka, Ioannis E. Saridakis & Angeliki Fotopoulou. 2014. Racism goes to the movies: a corpus-driven study of cross-linguistic racist discourse annotation and translation analysis. In Claudio Fantinuoli & Federico Zanettin (eds.), *New directions in corpus-based translation studies*, 31–61. Berlin: Language Science Press

This paper partly presents the first author's[1] ongoing PhD research, which aims to examine, from a descriptive viewpoint and by using corpus annotation, the translational norms of the socio-culturally marked discourse of racism, and the shifts observed during the discourse transfer from a source language (EN) into two target languages (EL, ES).[2] This paper focuses on the applied methodology, on the findings collected so far, and discusses problems and impediments observed during corpus analysis.

Racism, as manifested in discourse, is a constantly open issue that merits research (van Dijk 1993; Reisigl & Wodak 2001) and is clearly on the agenda of (critical) discourse analysis in light of the European social, political and economic backdrop. Realistic films on racism represent discourses emanating from racist stances, while cinema, as a medium widely accessible to the public communicates ideas apart from reflecting society. On the other hand, subtitles are considered to be among the most read translations and text types in countries with a subtitling tradition (Gottlieb 1997: 153 in Pedersen 2011: 125). To this end, the analysis of subtitles in racism-related films, rather than in films with sporadic racist utterances, seems to be better suited to research on the translation of racist-oriented discourse.

§2 of this article outlines the aims and scope of our research, and introduces the basic concepts and theoretical tenets used in this study. First, we introduce the principal discourse-related definitions of racism, together with a discussion of how racist discourse is handled by Critical Discourse Analysis. Subsequently, we provide a brief overview of Appraisal Theory, first developed by Martin & White (2005). This theory has been used extensively in sentiment analysis. Finally, we consider the phenomenon of register shifts in subtitles.

§3 presents our corpus-driven methodology and the corpus tools used in our research. §4 and §5 present and exemplify the implementation of our methodology and outline the principal findings with regard to context-bound register shifts in translation.

---

[1] The second author, I.E. Saridakis is the PhD research director. Dr. A. Fotopoulou also participates in the project's consultative committee. The authors express their gratitude to V. Giouli, scientific associate at the Institute for Language and Speech Processing (ILSP) for her support in initially developing and implementing the sentiment annotation scheme described in this paper, and in adopting the corpus metadata handling model used in our method.

[2] Batsalia & Sella-Mazi (2010: 120–121) define "shifts" as subsuming all changes that may appear during the translation process, on a semantic, lexical, morphological, syntactic, pragmatic, and/or stylistic level. The "translation shift" hypothesis is a useful and powerful descriptive device, to approach hermeneutically the phenomenon of differentiation of the TT from its ST, without stigmatising it.

2 Research aims and scope

The focus of our work is to examine racist discourse from a translation perspective, identifying its structure, its textual deployment, and its elements and traits on the basis of lexicogrammatical evidence and using a classificatory device. In other words, our aim is to examine how racist attitudes can be classified in spoken film discourse, linking this classification to the context of the utterances from which the text chunks have been drawn. This classification and analysis is based on a model adapted from Appraisal Theory (Martin & White 2005), using postulates derived from Critical Discourse Analysis (Reisigl & Wodak 2001; van Dijk 2000a; 2000b; 2002). Finally, by linking the examined ST utterances to their translations in two TLS, register shifts can be analysed on the basis of previous research (Hatim & Mason 1997; Mason 2001; Pettit 2005; Mubenga 2009; Munday 2012). This study is based on corpus resources and methodologies. We first constructed an ad hoc corpus and annotated it with a purpose-built annotation scheme, then set out to identify register shifts in the translation of racist utterances. This approach is exemplified by the preliminary findings reported in this article.

2.1 Background. Racism and racist discourse

The phenomenon of racism is fuzzy and evasive, and the term is often used rather vaguely, even to describe discriminatory phenomena other than those related to the concept of "race". *Racism* subsumes everyday practices and behaviours, both verbal and non-verbal, stereotyping, discriminatory practices, institutional systemic policies, or even acts of racial segregation and genocides (Giddens 2009: 637–653).

How racism is defined depends, in the final analysis, on the scope of individual research: for example, literature lists distinctive definitions such as "institutional" or "systemic" racism, to designate racism that is present in societal structures, such as the educational system or the police; "neo-racism" or "cultural racism" that draws from cultural differences in an attempt to provide explanations for inequalities and the actual position of ethnic minorities, immigrants and refugees in society, as opposed to the "old-style" and merely biologically explained racism that is based on physical characteristics to sustain the inferiority of certain group members; "everyday racism" as a common societal behaviour; or racism as part of the wider phenomenon of "heterophobia", the fear of the Other, that gives birth to various forms of discrimination (Essed 1991; Reisigl & Wodak 2001; Memmi 2000: 118). Racism has "the cognitive function of organizing the social representations (attitudes, knowledge) of the group, and thus of indirectly monitor[ing] the group-related social practices, and hence also the text and talk of members" (van Dijk 1995: 248).

We share Van Dijk's position that ideologies are systems with both a cognitive and a social dimension, in other words "belief systems" that involve ideas, judgements, values and attitudes shared by members of social groups and targeting other social groups.

2.2 Racism in Critical Discourse Analysis and Corpus Linguistics

Racist discourse has been investigated mainly within the framework of Critical Discourse Analysis (CDA). It has been shown that racist discourse *about* and *addressed at* minorities and immigrants tends to use the following means: lexicon and especially referential and predicative strategies; syntax, i.e. use of passive instead of active voice; rhetorical devices such as metaphors, metonymies and connotations (*synecdoches*); argument schemata; pragmatic features; recurrent topics concerning differences mainly in terms of habits, culture, language or religion of others, or even representations of others as a threat for "our" jobs, safety and culture; standard arguments and fallacies; and local moves or intensifying and mitigation strategies (Reisigl & Wodak 2001; van Dijk 2000a; 2000b; 2002).

In a study developing along lines that are ideationally and hermeneutically analogous to the study reported in this paper, Baker et al. (2008) have effectively used a Corpus Linguistics approach to analyse a large corpus of news articles about refugees, asylum seekers, immigrants and migrants and have shown that such an empirical approach can fruitfully combine CL and CDA.[3]

2.3 Appraisal Theory and Sentiment Analysis

Appraisal Theory is a model that has evolved within the theoretical framework of Systemic Functional Linguistics. It "is concerned with the interpersonal in language, with the subjective presence of writers/speakers in texts as they adopt stances towards both the material they present and those with whom they communicate [...], with how writers/speakers approve and disapprove, enthuse and abhor, applaud and criticise, and with how they position their readers/listeners

---

[3] Research in the field of CADS, or Corpus-Assisted Discourse Studies focuses on the use of corpora and corpus analysis techniques, so as to unveil meaning and style in discourse and to examine particular discourses. For a comprehensive bibliography on CADS compiled by C. Gabrielatos, see: http://goo.gl/WHB2mh.

to do likewise" (Martin & White 2005: 1). In addition, appraisal "co-articulates interpersonal meaning"[4] (Martin & White 2005: 33), reflecting the speakers' social roles and interpersonal positioning, and their inter-subjective negotiation. It is an approach that can be used to explore, describe and explain how language is used to express stances.[5]

The Appraisal framework has been widely used in Sentiment Analysis to identify subjective information, emotions and opinions, as manifested in discourse (see e.g. Whitelaw, Garg & Argamon 2005; Taboada & Grieve 2004; Asher, Benamara & Mathieu 2009) and to classify the attitude of speakers/writers. More recently, this type of analysis has been applied in translation research (see the work reported in Munday 2012: 42–79), with the aim to "describe the different components of a reader's attitude, the strength of that attitude (graduation) and the ways that the speaker aligns him/herself with the sources of attitude and with the receiver (engagement)" (Munday 2012: 2).

The three sub-components of Appraisal (theory) are *attitude, graduation* and *engagement. Attitude* is concerned with affect, judgement and appreciation and has a polarity, i.e., a positive or a negative dimension. *Engagement* deals with the positioning of the speaker towards the evaluation and concerns the rhetorical devices that are used to vary the engagement of speakers with their utterances (*I believe..., it is rumoured that..., X said....*). *Graduation* concerns grading phenomena and adjusting the degree of evaluations (e.g., in the grading between competent player, good player, brilliant player or contentedly, happily, joyously, ecstatically). Moreover, graduation is applicable also to indicators of engagement. A bare assertion does not have the same intensity as an utterance that is introduced with a modal value, such as *possibly* or *certainly* or presented as a hypothesis (compare the following sentences as to the grade of engagement they

---

[4] According to Halliday (1978: 112), "the interpersonal component represents the speaker's meaning potential as an intruder. It is the participatory function of language, language as doing something". Through the interpersonal component, the speaker places himself in the context of the situation, to express also "his own attitudes and judgements" and thus to seek to "influence the attitudes and behaviours of others" (ibid.). In other words, the interpersonal meaning can be defined as the one deriving from the roles and relationships, e.g. status, intimacy, contact, sharedness between interactants (Eggins & Slade 1997: 49). Finally, for Kress (2010: 94), meaning-making is "both social and external and social and internal [...] Meaning is constantly created in a transformative process of interactions with and in response to the prompts of social others and of the culturally shaped environment; and there is constant 'internal' action, an (inner) response in constant engagement with the world".

[5] In this context, *stance* is meant to represent "performances through which speakers may align or disalign themselves with and/or ironize stereotypical associations with particular linguistic forms" (Jaffe 2009: 4).

represent: *They're all a bunch of fucking freeloaders. Some of them are all right I guess*) (see Martin & White 2005: 136 for detailed examples of how graduation applies to attitudinal meanings and engagement values).

2.4 Subtitling: Analysis of register shifts

The ultimate aim of this study is to analyse register shifts in subtitled films. Munday suggests that "*major shifts in key attitudinal markers are not likely to occur except perhaps in certain genres* [...] *where the* TL *conventions are strongest*" (Munday 2012: 159–160; our emphasis) and calls for the inclusion of Appraisal Theory in the study of how the interpersonal meaning is materialised in translation (ibid.). Munday regards evaluative expressions in text as critical points that pose problems for translators/interpreters and which are especially susceptible to translators' interventions: he investigates the way a translator's subjective stance is manifested by shifts in translations and concludes that translation choices indicate "both an ideological and axiological position" (Munday 2012: 155). The translator is a critical reader of the original, and he/she is likely either to reproduce the ideological stance of the source text by complying with its general orientation, oppose it by resisting its ideological postulates, or to both reproduce and rework the source in a more tactical approach that repositions the audience in relation to the writer (Munday 2012: 157). Such stance-taking attitudes on the part of the translator–as–critical–reader depend on the overall evaluative prosody of the text, the value of which "the translator sometimes feels obliged to explicate [...] in the interests of the target audience" (ibid.). On a more theoretical line of thought, Batsalia & Sella-Mazi (2010: 215) relate register to style, and speak of stylistic shifts in translation. These are considered to be changes of the language level(s) (i.e. lexical, semantic, pragmatic or morphosyntactic) that can be mapped to stylistic choices. Such choices derive from the translator's own perception of the potential offered by the system of the TL and of the stylistic habits governing the text genre at hand, in a given language. More in particular, subtitling research can optimally incorporate discourse analysis techniques, so as to depict the mechanism through which racism is reflected on cinematographic discourse.

The interpersonal dimension of discourse has been explored using various models in subtitling research. Hatim & Mason (1997: 78–96) and Mason (2001) have drawn attention to translation shifts that relate to the interpersonal dynamics of film characters, pointing out that tenor is the metafunction of discourse, which is frequently sacrificed in subtitles. Their analytical approach is that of interpersonal pragmatics, with a focus on politeness features and face-threatening acts. They compare source and target texts using a qualitative method with examples from French films translated into English. On the other hand, Pettit (2005) analyses subtitled and dubbed French versions of two English films, with the aim to examine whether the registers presented in these films are maintained or discarded in the respective subtitled and dubbed versions, providing a variety of examples of formal and informal registers, including slang and sophisticated language. Finally, Mubenga (2009) proposes a multi-modal pragmatic analysis using an SFL approach, which takes into account three components (visual, functional and cognitive) and three levels of analysis (ideational, interpersonal, textual). While sharing the basic assumptions of the above-mentioned studies, our work focuses on register shifts within a specific type of discourse, i.e. racist discourse. Also, in line with Munday (2012), it relies on Appraisal Theory to classify the translators' stance-taking tendencies. We use corpus linguistic techniques to explore translation shifts, by comparing source and target texts in two language pairs.

This study first makes extensive use of linguistic annotation to analyse translational behaviour and to investigate register shifts that take place in racist discourse; subsequently, it validates the data using large monolingual reference corpora. Based on a thorough examination of concordance lines, it provides an analysis of cross-linguistic patterns and of the collocational strength of the lexemes examined.

The aim of cross-linguistic analysis is thus to observe how and to which extent translators have addressed the categories of attitudes, relying on the annotation of register shifts. Using the GATE annotation system (Cunningham et al. 2002), register shifts were classified as *neutral transfer, over-toning, under-toning,* and *possible change of register category.* This allowed for the retrieval of bilingual segments containing examples of these shifts.

3 Corpus methodology

3.1 Corpus description

For the purpose of the present research we have developed a relatively small-scale translational film corpus consisting of the transcriptions of the dialogues of five films in English and their Greek and Spanish subtitles.[6]

---

[6] The corpus forms part of the Metashare initiative launched by ELDA (see: metashare.elda.org). Details on the linguistic resource (Multilingual aligned corpus of subtitles annotated for sentiment) can be found at http://goo.gl/o45NK5.

The criteria used for the design of the corpus relate to the sociolinguistic situation and communicative functions (Saridakis 2010: 49–52) of the target population and can be summarised as follows:

- all films are feature films, belonging to the drama genre;
- they were all produced between 1989 and 2006 and the frame of reference of their plot is contemporary;
- their story revolves around racism and inter-racial relations;
- their approach to events and the depiction of characters have a realistic perspective;
- they contain verbally expressed racism in conversations and/or in monologues.

The five films of the corpus are:

- *Do the Right Thing* (Lee 1989);
- *American History X* (Kaye 1998);
- *Monster's Ball* (Forster 2001);
- *Crash* (Haggis 2004);
- *This is England* (Meadows 2006).

The total playtime of the corpus films corresponds to approximately 9 hours of audiovisual material, which translates into 51,000 words of transcribed English dialogue and 29,700 and 35,900 words of Greek and Spanish subtitles, respectively.

A wide variety of situations involving racist instances is present in our corpus, including both racist discourse *directed* at ethnically different Others, and racist discourse *about* ethnically different Others (van Dijk 2004: 351), which equally concern our investigation. The fact that our data contain a significant amount of conversations in inter-racial environments and everyday situations allows us to examine racist discourse *directed at* Others, and overt racist discursive practices. Such features are not always present in corpora of other genres, e.g. in political and journalistic discourse where racism has been studied more extensively using authentic linguistic data.[7] Cinematographic discourse can be considered as closely representing spoken impromptu racist discourse, more specifically in utterances that are *directed straight at* Others. Moreover, the communicative scenario from which our samples have been gathered is perhaps the only one permitting the construction of a parallel corpus for the cross-linguistic study of racist discourse from the perspective of translation, given that collecting samples of spoken language from other scenarios is impracticable.

Greek and Spanish were chosen as target languages because their respective cultures share some common characteristics. During the last decades, Greece and Spain have progressively seen large irregular immigration flows from non-European states, as both countries are key entry-points to Europe. Based on 2013 statistical data, non-European immigrants in Greece and Spain represented respectively 5.96 percent and 6.45 percent of the total country's population.[8] It is noteworthy that, with the exception of Greece and Spain, only Italy experiences comparative immigration flows from non-European countries.[9] In other words, this phenomenon has had a marked impact on the linguistic behaviour (i.e. inter-personal meaning), and therefore on racist discourse, as delineated in this study. However, although immigration is considered to have triggered racist attitudes across Europe, a social survey on racism and xenophobia has shown that the Greek population has quite stronger negative attitudes towards minorities when compared to the Spanish population.[10] The phenomenon of immigration has had a marked impact on racist discourse and therefore on interpersonal meaning, as negotiated by linguistic behaviour.

A corpus-based approach facilitates the comparison of source and target segments and can help explore the extent of reflection on different socio-cultural realities and attitudes and the effect on the linguistic choices of subtitlers.

In terms of translation practices, previous work in the EL–ES language pair has *inter alia* shown that Greek subtitlers tend to omit repeated or redundant information to a more significant extent when compared to their Spanish counterparts (Sokoli 2009). In short, similar phenomena are bound to be related to generalised tendencies, and this can assist our effort in explicating the textual findings in our corpus.

---

[7] E.g., in the research reported in Baker et al. (2008); van Dijk (1993), etc.

[8] See: Eurostat 2014 data http://goo.gl/hbouLx.

[9] Cmp. Vasileva (2011: 4); and http://goo.gl/NnhjYR.

[10] See: Special Eurobarometer 2007. *Discrimination in the European Union* http://goo.gl/t9e6Gk.

3.1.1 Multimodality

Films are polysemiotic discourse events (Gottlieb 2005). The explication of the meaning of utterances cannot rely solely on the verbal component, but must also take into account its context: "Any consideration of film text in isolation from the context of the moving image and soundtrack is [...] doomed to failure" (Mason 2001: 23). The audiovisual text is expressed and completed through four semiotic channels (Zabalbeascoa 2008):

- audio-verbal (words uttered);

- audio-nonverbal (all other sounds);

- visual-verbal (writing);

- visual-nonverbal (all other visual signs).

Hence, there can be no valid analysis of the instances of racist discourse if the filmic message is not considered as a whole. The film provided the communicative context for each utterance and for the stance of each character which, additionally, is not static but can change as the plot unfolds. The actual use of the words and its pragmatic features can be deciphered only in this context. "Every clause [...] is a combination of ideational, interpersonal (identity and relational) and textual meanings [...] People make choices about the design and structure of their clauses which amount to choices about how to signify (and construct) social identities, social relationships, and knowledge and belief" (Fairclough 1992: 76). Even apparently innocent lexical choices can indicate a racist stance, while key lexical items are not necessarily racist: a typical example is probably the use of the word *nigger* as an indicator of *belonging* in an otherwise non-racist dialogue between black people:

> "You want to get killed, nigger?"
> (*Crash*, in a scene where a black male attempts an armed robbery against the driver of a luxury car and, to his surprise, the driver who resists, is also a black male).

In this case, the word itself retains its ideological profile and implications as a re-appropriated word. The connotation of key lexical words cannot be taken for granted *a priori* and out-of-context. This is because "the meaning of sentences, clauses, nouns, nominalisations and adjectives are all possible targets for the expression of ideological content, usually in the form of evaluative concepts. In all cases, however, such a semantic representation of opinions in attitudes or models *needs to be analysed in context*" (van Dijk 1995: 260; our emphasis).

Moreover, this corpus, comprised of transcribed (i.e. originally oral) STs and written TTs, can also be characterised as a compilation of inter-semiotic facts (Jakobson 2012) that imply an inherent change of the mode of the message. Thus, certain features of the ST, such as non-standard dialects or code-switching, are not expected to be present in the TT(s). Such features are not usually (or at least, not automatically) transferred to the TL (Hatim & Mason 1997: 78). This change implies also that some prosodic features of the source dialogues are not represented in the written subtitles. This holds true also for other non-verbal features, e.g. for gestures. Such features are elements of a semiotic system (the "paralanguage") that interrelates with language (Halliday & Matthiessen 2014: 32–42) and have been used in our analysis in order to properly contextualise and decode the meaning of the ST. However, it would be very difficult, and well outside the scope of this study, to trace whether and up to what point the SL and TL audiences decode them in the same way:

> "Modes differ in what they offer from culture to culture [...]: the different requirements of different societies and their members and the consequent different shaping. As a semiotic resource, *image* in one culture is therefore not identical to *image* in another. Even across closely related cultures and 'languages' (such as English, French, German) differences in the cultural use of, say, *vocal intensity* (appearing as *accent* in words and as *rhythm* in extended speech) or of *pitch variation* (appearing as intonation); differences of pace, of *vocalic quality*, and so on, lead to characteristic variation in meanings made, in signs" (Kress 2010: 81; emphasis in the original).

3.2 Corpus tools

We orthographically transcribed the English dialogues and, using ELAN (Brugman & Russell 2004), aligned all utterances to the corresponding translated Greek and Spanish subtitles. ELAN is a tool designed for complex annotations of video and audio resources. It allows the use of multiple layers of annotation, which are attributed to each speaker and are time-aligned. In other words, the transcript is aligned to the Greek and Spanish subtitles available in the DVD distributions of the films, thus making the corpus a *star corpus*, i.e. source texts in one language, and their aligned texts in multiple target languages (Johansson 2003: 140–141; Saridakis 2010: 260). As shown in Figure 1, the corpus can be expanded to include more target languages in the future, to allow for further cross-linguistic investigations of the translational phenomena. Each utterance is accompanied by a time marker pointing to the corresponding "time-slot" in the film. ELAN allows also the inclusion of metadata to tag the speakers of individual utterances and exports text in TEI-compliant XML format using the TEI-Drop application (Schmidt 2011), and thus ensures interoperability with the applications used in subsequent stages of our research. The investigator can access the exact point of each utterance, detect the scene from which each utterance has been extracted and reconstruct the communicative context, so as to properly interpret it.

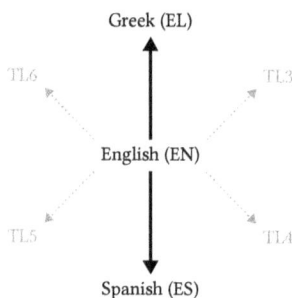

Greek (EL)

TL6   TL3

English (EN)

TL5   TL4

Spanish (ES)

Figure 1: The "star" layout of the study corpus

Concerning the description of the corpus contents, the following metadata has been used (based on the TEI guidelines):

- for files (in the file header section): the audio and video file name/path, the film title, the publication statement (information concerning the distribution of the text);

- for utterances: information on the speaker (e.g., SPK1 [Danny]), the time-stamp (*anchorsynch*), and the dependent/aligned tiers with the Greek and Spanish translations respectively (*spanGrp* type).

An example of an XML-tagged utterance and of its translations into EL and ES, as outputted from ELAN following processing in TEI-Drop, is in Figure 2.

ELAN is used to visualise each utterance in its context, together with the speaker and the aligned subtitled utterances.

To manually annotate the corpus, we have used the GATE platform (Cunningham et al. 2002).[11] The annotation was performed on the level of text chunks,

---

[11] The annotation methodology and a preliminary annotation scheme (regarding emotions) were first presented in Mouka et al. (2012). The annotation scheme used in this paper was later finalised and has been reported in Mouka (2014).

```
<div>
<u who="\#_SPK1">
<anchor synch="\#_T3497"/>
"We_are_not_enemies,_but_friends.
<anchor_synch="\# T3498"/>
</u>
<spanGrp_type="subtitles el">
<span_to="\#T 3498"_from="\# T3497">"Δεν είμαστεεχθροί , αλλάφίλοι .</
    span> </spanGrp>
<spanGrp type="subtitles_es">
<span to="\#T_3498" from="\#_T3497">"No_somos_enemigos,_sino_amigos.</
    span>_</spanGrp>
</div>
```

Figure 2: Example of an XML-tagged utterance

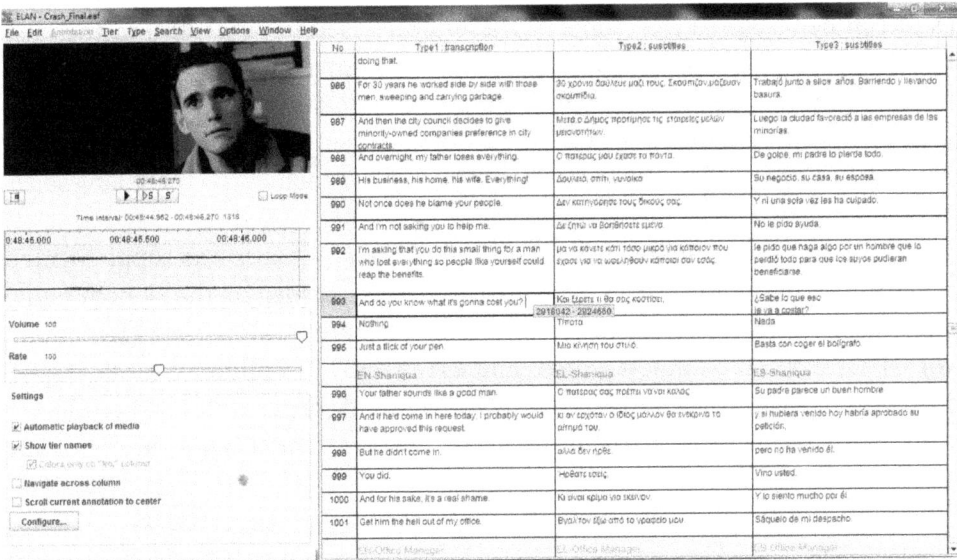

Figure 3: ELAN interface, in transcription mode

i.e. of extended units of meaning (Sinclair 1996). GATE is optimally designed for linguistic annotation. Even though ELAN can also be used for linguistic annotation, it would not be adequate for processing multiple speakers' conversations. ELAN has been primarily developed for psycholinguistic research and each layer of annotation depends on the principal layer attributed to a single speaker. This would be impracticable in the case of our corpus. The change of tool has made impossible the direct access to the audiovisual material and necessitated the simultaneous use of both platforms.

3.3 Reference corpora

Although the context of situation provides the main clues on how/why words are used in a specific utterance and what was really meant by it, it cannot be reasonably argued that there is one and only one meaning in each utterance, or a single and precisely determined stance, nor that such meaning or stance can be fully and indisputably perceived and decoded by the analyst. This also applies to our effort to distinguish racist-oriented from neutral discourse elements. What one considers as being blatantly racist or has "labelled" as politically incorrect may be considered "neutral" by others. While well-known racial slurs, such as the lexeme *nigger*, are marked as offensive in all contemporary dictionaries, it can be observed that some of these terms used to be neutral in the past. In order to avoid – as far as possible – being influenced by preconceptions and personal beliefs, especially in view of the cross-linguistic nature of the investigation, the interpretation of how racist markers are used in discourse was based on the evidence provided by reference corpora, one for each of the three languages considered.[12]

In the comparative analysis the intuition of the annotator was supplemented with the interpretation of data from the corpora pre-loaded on the SketchEngine platform (Kilgarriff et al. 2004).[13] These corpora are: enTenTen12 (11+ billion words), GkWaC (124 million words) and esTenTen11 (2.1 billion words), respectively for English, Greek and Spanish.[14] The selected corpora offer texts collected from the Web and, as such, include a variety of text genres and a variety of lan-

---

[12] "Reference corpora [...] can be used as benchmarks for special corpora. Whenever we do not want to look at standard language as a whole but at some special phenomenon we happen to be interested in, we usually have to compile a corpus that fits our research focus" (Teubert & Čermáková 2007: 68). In Translation Studies, the use of reference corpora as discourse benchmarks is exemplified, *inter alia*, in Kenny (1998: 516).

[13] www.sketchengine.co.uk.

[14] For a definition of the TenTen collection of corpora, see Jakubíček et al. (2013).

guage uses (both formal and informal). Furthermore, the SketchEngine system allows the visualisation of an extended co-text of concordances. Web corpora also include authentic texts that have not been stylistically filtered and can thus present higher frequencies of informal language, slang and insulting words compared to other general reference corpora (e.g., in the case of Greek, the Corpus of Greek Texts/SEK[15] and the Hellenic National Corpus/HNC[16]), which usually comprise only authoritative texts or texts that have previously been published in printed form or broadcast and, in that sense, have undergone pre-print editing and perhaps been subjected to cultural and linguistic "filtering" prior to their publication. In most cases, the content of such general reference corpora is "mainstream"/standard texts.[17]

4 Corpus annotation: Analysis and examples

4.1 Implementing the Appraisal Theory

This study focuses on the "negative" expressions of racism, i.e., on the discoursal emphasis on negative and/or de-emphasis of positive "things" about *Them*, of which there are many in the corpus. It is beyond our scope to examine the emphasis on positive things and/or the de-emphasis of negative things about *Us*, although these are, more often than not, the other side of the same coin (van Dijk 2000b: 44).

For the purposes of our work we have partially adapted the Appraisal Theory model by focusing on the classification and "graduation" of attitudes, including the graduation of engagement features, which are labelled "strength" in our schema. Thus, strength is linked to:

- the valence of an evaluation and its intensification/mitigation; and

- the intensity of the speaker's engagement with the evaluation, given that our focus is on the degree of the negative attitude expressed by the speaker as a whole.

---

[15] SEK is provided by the University of Athens http://sek.edu.gr.

[16] HNC is provided by the Institute for Language and Speech Processing (ILSP) http://hnc.ilsp.gr.

[17] Teubert & Čermáková (2007: 65–66), referring to English, define its "standard" form as corresponding to the "private annual reading load of educated middle class citizens" and go on to describe a possible formulation of this definition, in corpus design terms. Such an analogy could also be made for Greek, even though it is not always clear or substantiated how the textual sub-categories would be included in such a corpus.

The attitude types used are summarised as follows:

- *Affect*: emotions and emotional reactions;

- *Judgement*: evaluation of behaviours;

- *Appreciation*: evaluation of phenomena, including aesthetics.

Our main focus is therefore on exploring the interpersonal nature, the tenor of the discourse and the social relations of the characters of the films, as far as racist stances are manifested in discourse, elements of which are the evaluation of behaviours and situations and the expression of negative emotions and opinions (see Fotopoulou et al. 2009). In this sense, we have categorised and manually annotated "[a]ttitudes [...] divided into three regions of feeling, 'affect', 'appreciation' and 'judgement'" (Martin & White 2005: 35–43).

For the purposes of our analysis, we annotated every segment of racist attitude of the film characters (appraisers) that express negative evaluations towards a person or a group of another ethnicity/"race"/religion (appraised entity). All candidate instances are interpreted and classified as instantiations of a type of attitude towards "Others". In this sense, the utterance *Minorities don't give two shits about this country* (American History X), taken semantically, simply informs us about the indifference (affect) of minorities towards *this country*. However, considering how it is used in the given context, we focus on the interlocutor's intended meaning, which is to implicitly criticise the members of minorities as indifferent free-loaders who just want to exploit the country. Therefore, it is annotated as an implicit judgement.

4.2 Attitude types and usage perspective

A systematic classification of racist attitudes requires the clearest possible definition for each category, since the boundaries among attitude types are not always accurate and undoubted. This is not surprising, given that "[i]n a general sense, affect, judgement, and appreciation all encode feeling" (Martin 2000: 147). It cannot be argued that negative judgements or appreciations bear no traces/nuances of affect and that speakers can either express emotions or judge. As a matter of fact, "[a]ffect can perhaps be taken as the basic system [...]" (ibid.), as an immanent or emerging characteristic of every attitude. Through this perspective, "[a]s judgement, affect is re-contextualised as an evaluation matrix for behaviour [...] [a]s appreciation, affect is re-contextualised as an evaluation matrix for the products of behaviour (and wonders of nature)" (Martin 2000: 147).

In this sense, we have annotated as instances of *affect* all expressions of emotions, as signs of emotional reactions of the characters related to the specific discourse type. Further, *appreciation* was defined as evaluations, mainly aesthetic, of humans as entities, as evaluations not related to their behaviour but to their characteristics such as colour, ethnicity, religion, physical characteristics and supposed inherent characteristics. Such assessments are negative markers of difference. Finally, *judgement* which "deals with attitudes towards behaviour, which we admire or criticise, praise or condemn" (Martin & White 2005: 42) applies to cases that can be defined as rationalisations of a fact or as reflecting a causal relation between things or facts. On the contrary, in *appreciation*, the speaker's stance is intuitive or dogmatic, i.e. non-refutable in the specific context of situation. In our opinion, this formalisation defines more objectively the classification of attitudes compared to the broader and more inclusive definition offered by Martin & White (2005: 42–45).

The basic tri-fold categorisation of attitude as applied in this study is as follows:

- *Affect*: characterises negative emotions and emotional reactions towards Others, principally instances that are indicative of hate and anger based on or evoked by racial/ethnic/religious differences.

- *Appreciation*: characterises negative evaluations of Others based on their inherent characteristics, or on characteristics that are presented as such, dogmatically used as sufficient reasons for negative evaluations.

- *Judgement*: characterises negative evaluations of the behaviour of Others, judged as people that act in relation to their racial/ethnic/religious difference.

In the paragraphs below, these types are exemplified.

4.2.1 Affect

(1) Your mother, she *hated them niggers* too (*Monster's Ball*)

(2) That means *not welcome* (*American History X*) [utterance addressed to a Jew while the speaker reveals his swastika tattoo]

(3) Take your fucking pizza piece and *go the fuck back to Africa* (*Do the Right Thing*)

(4) Yeah, *fuck off, you Paki bastards* (*This is England*)

(5) *What the hell are those niggers* doing out there? (*Monster's Ball*)

4.2.2 Appreciation

(6) We'll let the *niggers, kikes and spics* grab for their piece of the pie (*American History X*)

(7) *A bunch of people* who *aren't even citizens of this country* [...] (*American History X*)

(8) She *smells like fish and chips and guacamole* (*American History X*)

(9) Three and a half million of us, who can't find fucking work because *they're taking them all, because it's fucking cheap labour* (*American History X*)

(10) How come *niggers are so stupid?* (*Do the Right Thing*)

(11) Magic, Eddie, Prince, are not *niggers.* I mean, they're not *black,* I mean... (*Do the Right Thing*)

4.2.3 Judgement

(12) Look at these little *fucking sewer rats* (*This is England*) [referring to young immigrants playing in a yard]

(13) *Immigration,* AIDS, *welfare, those are problems of the black community, the Hispanic community, the Asian community* (*American History X*)

(14) One in every three black males is in some phase of the correctional system. Is that a coincidence or do these people *have like a racial commitment to crime?* (*American History X*)

(15) All right. Well, you know what I can't do? I can't look at you without thinking about the *five or six more qualified white men who didn't get your job* (*Crash*)

(16) He's one of those *proud to be nigger people* (*American History X*)

Although "interpersonal epithets" (see Halliday & Matthiessen 2014: 376–377), e.g. evaluative adjectives, are the most obvious evaluative device of language, the lexico-grammatical choices that express attitude are infinite, especially if we consider that evaluative uses of language can be present in discourse both explicitly and implicitly (see Munday 2012: 23). As shown in the above examples, the lexico-grammatical means to express attitude are vast and not limited to closed semantic or grammatical categories.

In addition, phenomena investigated from another point of view in previous studies are also evident in our data, but are further analysed as instantiations of evaluative attitudes. Referential/nomination strategies and predication strategies, such as racial slurs and metaphors (*sewer rats*) analysed by Reisigl & Wodak (2001) as a means to categorise membership, are analysed here as evidences of the speaker's stance. Thus, we observe the presence of racial slurs, such as *nigger*, in all three types of attitude:

- used to express mere anger and hate, as in (1) and (5),

- used in appreciations just to refer to Others in a disparaging manner, presenting the fact of belonging to other racial groups and/or having their "inherent" characteristics as being *per se* negative, as in (6) and (11), or

- used in judgements to negatively evaluate a certain person's behaviour, which is presented as related to the fact that he/she is black (12).

The interpretation of each instance is based on the context of situation, and is further based on the presence of various markers, either explicitly stated, as in (1) where the verb *hate* is used, or using interjections such as *go the fuckback, fuck off* and *what the hell* [in (3), (4), and (5)].

On the other hand, in (6) racial slurs are used instead of "neutral" ethnic denominations as disparaging terms, simply to mark the inferiority of the mentioned groups. The utterance in example (11) is a response to the interlocutor's argument that, despite his constant negative attitude towards black people, all his favourite celebrities (Eddie Murphy, Magic Johnson and Prince) are black. It is a representative example of how a highly marked racial slur is used as a negative appreciation, to evaluate people as being "nice" or "bad".

Accordingly, our data includes many convictions and stereotyped visions of Others (7) and recurrent topics or *topoi*, as "common-sense reasoning [that is] typical for specific issues" (van Dijk 2000c in Baker et al. 2008: 299, note 21; see also Reisigl & Wodak 2001: 74–76). Examples are the *topos* of finance (9), the *topos* of threat (13, 14) and the *topos* of justice or equal opportunities (15). Such visions can be used as appreciations or judgements, i.e. presented as either negative phenomena, as in (9), or as criticism of the behaviour of Others, as in (13), (14) and (15).

4.2.4 Type overlaps

As mentioned already, it is normal that the boundaries between categories are not always clear-cut: thus, in cases that could belong to more than one category, we have used double annotation: this is both methodologically permissible and of course technically possible. This allows for a subsequent analysis on both levels, e.g. of *affect* and *appreciation*, for the sake of contrastive analysis within the two categories, and hence for further refining the classification/annotation scheme.

(17) You *gold-teeth, gold-chain-wearing, fried-chicken and biscuit-eating monkey, ape, baboon, big-thigh, fast running, high-jumping, spear chucking, 360-degree basketball-dunking, titsoon, spade, moulignon!*

In this sense, according to our definition of attitudes, the utterance in (17) used by an Italian-American in an aggressive manner to express hatred directed to a black person, shows negative affect. At the same time, the long list of epithets enumerated represent appreciations referring to his interlocutor.

4.3 *Attitude features*

Attitudes are also analysed in terms of their features.

4.3.1 Implicit and explicit attitudes

As mentioned above, we always categorise attitudes expressed towards persons or groups of other ethnicities/"races"/religions. In many cases, attitudes are not explicitly stated in the text, but evoked, expressed implicitly. Such an interpretation can rely on common knowledge, on the co-text and on the context of the situation.

> "If by expressing meaning A, language users (also) mean B, such an implication can be reconstructed by recipients only on the basis of inferences from culturally shared knowledge of language meanings (e.g. as represented in the lexicon of the language) or more generally on the basis of shared knowledge, including particular knowledge about the knowledge of the speaker" (van Dijk 1995: 168).

Thus, in example (8) above, one should know that *fish and chips and guacamole* refer to the culinary traditions of Latin Americans in order to properly interpret it, whereas in example (12) knowledge about the policies of affirmative action against racial discrimination in the USA is crucial in order to interpret the utterance correctly. Moreover, in example (12) the term *sewer rat* is used metaphorically to designate useless people that cause problems to society.

4.3.2 Irony

Irony is also a case of implicit meaning, a pragmatic phenomenon used to express a meaning contrary or different to the literal one. Once again, its recognition depends on the situational context which indicates something different than the apparent meaning of the utterance, the speaker's tone of voice or the "interpreters' assumptions about the beliefs or values of the text producer" (Fairclough 1992: 123). For instance, the utterance in example 18 is used to depreciate African-American literature:

(18) What is it, Black History Month? (*American History X*)

4.3.3 Indirect/Direct attitudes

Some utterances do not express a racist attitude but are still indicative of the social roles of the participants and can reflect racism as internalised.[18] These are cases where speakers comment the racist stance of others and are annotated as indirect references to racist attitudes.

(19) Man's singing about lynching niggers. "Gonna buy me a rope and lynch me a nigger" (*Crash*)

(20) Your partner's a racist prick (*Crash*)

4.3.4 Polarity

Polarity refers to the positive or negative dimension of an attitude, distinguishing positive from negative affect, appreciation or judgement. As mentioned already, for the aims of our study we focus on negative instances.

---

[18] *Internalised racism* is defined as the situation in which individuals, groups and cultures that have been subjected to racism and oppression, shift this racism to oppress themselves and others who have experienced racism and discrimination (Lawrence 2002: 92).

4.3.5 Strength

The strength of each instance is taken into account and an indication of low, medium or high valence is given to each instance. Admittedly, this is the most subjective parameter of our effort, so that in order to decide on the strength of an utterance inter-subjective agreement among the annotators was required in most cases. The collocational behaviour of the lexemes examined was assessed with the help of the English reference corpus.

4.4 Annotation scheme overview

The attitude classification outlined above and used as annotation scheme in the reported project can be schematised in Figure 4.

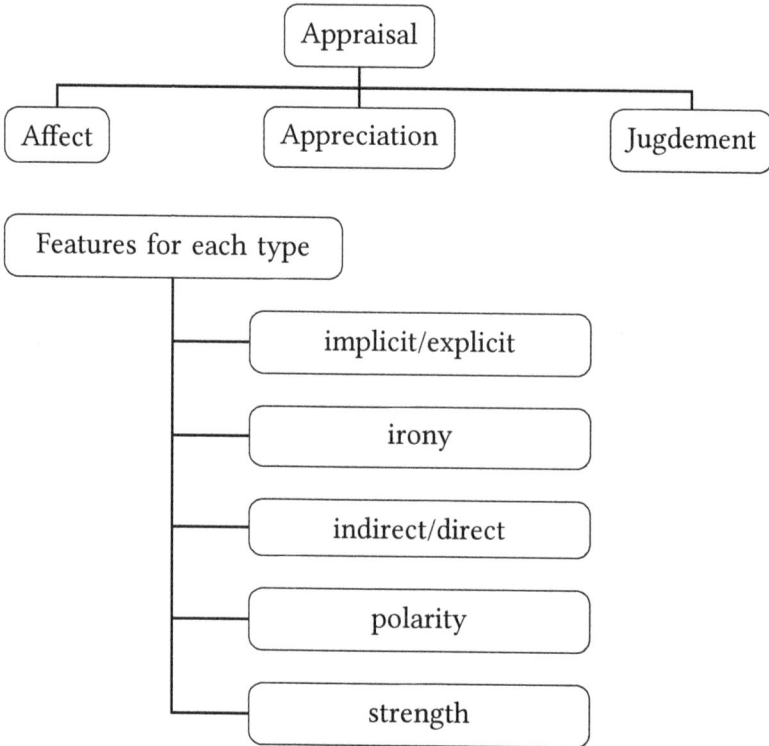

Figure 4: Corpus annotation scheme

5 Register shifts: Analysis and examples

This study investigates how racist/heterophobic discourse is transferred when a film is translated into socio-cognitively distinct and somewhat remote linguistic systems. It tries to systematise changes of tenor (Halliday 1978) in translation by means of a comprehensive classification of attitudes and their cross-linguistic mapping.

We therefore believe that retrodictively (von Wright 1971; Chesterman 2008) the diachronic study of discourse features, and more generally of racism, in translation could also benefit from such a hermeneutic approach. In the examples below, the shifts observed in discourse transfer have been explained in the light of the relationship between participants in discourse.

5.1 Examples

(*Examples 21–24 are sourced from American History X; examples 25-27 are sourced from Crash.*)

(21)   [EN] And now some fucking Korean owns it who fired *these guys* and is making a killing because he hired *40 fucking border jumpers*

[EL] Τώρα το 'χει ένας Κορεάτης, που απέλυσε τους *δικούς μας* και θησαυρίζει επειδή προσέλαβε *λαθρομετανάστες*

[Back translation] Now a Korean owns it who fired *our guys* and is making a killing because he hired *illegal immigrants*

Derek, a young skinhead, gives a speech to the rest of the gang members, trying to convince them to attack a supermarket owned by immigrants. Throughout his speech, negative attitudes towards immigrants are abundant. Among other arguments, he uses a variety of *topoi* as in, e.g. *immigrants take our jobs*. He uses rather colloquial expressions and the register of his speech is highly informal, indicative of the brotherhood relations among the in-groups. In terms of Appraisal Theory, this utterance is considered to be a highly marked negative judgement about immigrants.

If we concentrate on the last part of the utterance, that is *40 fucking border jumpers* and its respective Greek version rendered as *λαθρομετανάστες*, we notice immediately that the strength of the judgement is significantly altered. A closer look at each component of the TL unit of meaning reveals that *border jumper*, an apparently neutral term describing an action, is used as a depreciative, non-fixed, and possibly colloquial, synecdoche of *immigrants of Hispanic/Mexican origin*. An analysis of the term in enTenTen12 has returned only 57 hits of *border jumper(s)*, i.e. a negligible frequency in the enTenTen12 corpus (0.0 per million). Furthermore, as an analysis of the concordance lines reveals (see Figure 5, below), the term is used almost exclusively in a negative and highly disparaging sense (*border jumpers want our wealth*; *drug smugglers, human traffickers, border jumpers and other assorted criminals*; *border jumpers are slapping those legal immigrants*). Moreover, the presence of *fucking* (in the cluster *fucking border jumpers*), as an intensifier, as well as the emphatic mention to the number of immigrants employed, reinforce the overall negative prosody of the judgement, making it highly negative. On the other hand, the Greek translation of the utterance is limited to λαθρομετανάστες [clandestine immigrants], which is a generic term with no real connotation about the specific origin of the immigrants in question. By contrast, in GkWaC, the term λαθρομετανάστης has a frequency of 5.9 per million and its "ideologically neutral" synonym παράνομος μετανάστης[19] appears with a frequency of 0.7 per million. As to its usage profile, the term in question appears in various text genres and, most importantly, belongs to "standard" Greek as it is present in authoritative language.[20] The rendition of the utterance in Greek is a translation shift, in both field and tenor. The judgment loses its strength and maintains only the negative nuance inferred by the context of situation, as well as by the invented contrastive relation (Fairclough 2003: 87–89), i.e. by the contrast between δικούς μας 'our guys' and λαθρομετανάστες 'illegal immigrants', that has been added explicitly in the TT.

(22)   [EN] I mean, Christ, Lincoln *freed the slaves*, what, like hundred and thirty years ago. *How long does it take to get your act together?*

[EL] Ο Λίνκολν *απελευθέρωσε τους σκλάβους* πριν 130 χρόνια. *Πόσον καιρό χρειάζεσαι για να γίνεις άνθρωπος;*

[Back translation] Lincoln *freed the slaves* a hundred and thirty years ago. How long does it take to become a human?

During a family dinner, Derek argues with his professor (who apparently has an affair with his mother) about riots in the black neighbourhoods. Example (22)

---

[19] The use of the prefix "λαθρο-" (a derivative of the adjective λαθραίος clandestine, smuggled) to designate economic or political immigrants has been criticised by human rights and political organisations as being negatively loaded, even though this is not always the case, since language economy, not surprisingly, seems to opt for the single-word designator (λαθρομετανάστης) rather than for the presumably more neutral two-word unit (παράνομοςμετανάστης). This is apparent also in the concordances derived from GkWaC, where most occurrences do not have a negative connotation. The neutral (and hence stabilised as politically correct) designator παράνομος (illegal) is used instead by the administration.

[20] See above, note 17.

Query border, jumper **57** (0.0 per million)

Page 1   of 3   Go   Next | Last

doc#109056	since there are other ways of identifying border jumpers , such as "the kind of dress ... right down
doc#171898	identifiable (Muslims in Russia, Hispanic border jumpers in the US), both are unified (at least
doc#625986	my mind. Profiling? Well, when the border jumpers are coming in from Mexico it shouldn't
doc#629656	because of the criminal prosecution of repeat border jumpers . ... "it's unclear ... [whether]
doc#666369	himself important. That must remind you of border jumpers . AJ Libertarian Le:
doc#1011415	in the common law status of "outlawry." Border jumpers and immigrants who want our wealth and
doc#1337820	taking jobs. We need to quit focusing on border jumpers and look at the real problem. As stated
doc#2219845	had enough of nobody doing anything about border jumpers : Source: Los Angeles to boycott Arizona
doc#3395787	known fence breach points" as a signal to border jumpers . Other seemingly innocent activitie
doc#3442825	shout. Not wishing to be hauled in as a border jumper , Holmdahl leaped into the frigid Rio Grande
doc#3498887	mexico sends its millions of illegal alien border jumpers to invade the U.S., cry "racism", pose
doc#3658404	aforementioned drug smugglers, human traffickers border jumpers and other assorted criminals. I wonder
doc#5057516	identified that NSW had the highest number of border jumpers in 2002-2003. In total, 125,195 people
doc#5206024	immigration reforms go through and stopping the border jumpers . Rather than fill up a country that is
doc#5607550	prohibited from enforcing the law to stop these border jumpers , your families in Plainsville, Ohio, or
doc#5811734	worked very hard to get in here legally. Border jumpers are slapping those legal immigrants in
doc#5987724	the transit situation in which would-be border jumpers are retained blurs the distinction between
doc#6113973	borders are all but non-existent, and if a border jumper happens to stake their claim in this country
doc#6375465	target undocumented illegal immigrants and border jumpers . Government officials from South
doc#6788903	border? Where do all the illegal Zimbabwean border jumpers go to find jobs in South Africa? Why do

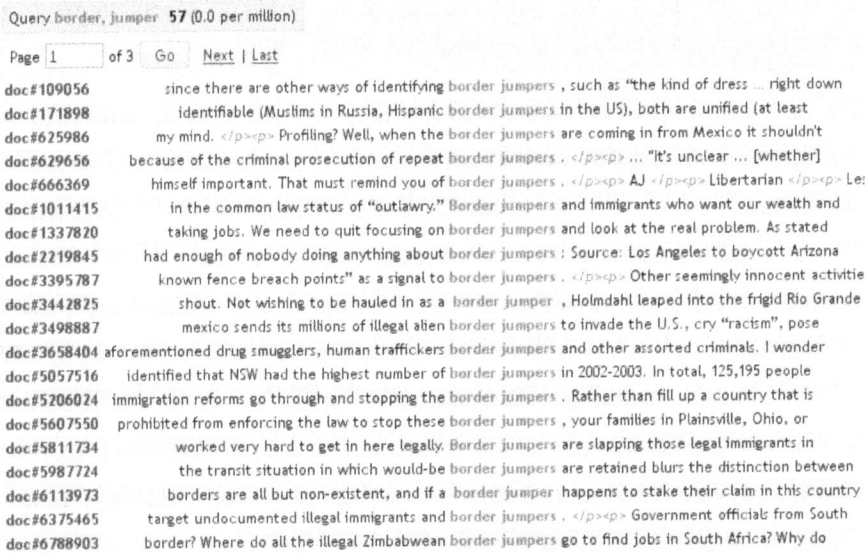

Figure 5: Concordance lines, *border jumpers*, GkWaC, in SketchEngine

comes to reinforce his argument that the sheer number of jailed black people proves their racial commitment to crime. The idiom used in this example, *get one's act together*, has the meaning of getting organised and being on schedule. The utterance is implicitly ironic. In our study, the source segment has been noted as a negative judgement of medium strength, this being mainly due to the ironic nature of both the argument and the reference to the end of slavery. On the other hand, the Greek translation uses the idiom γίνομαι άνθρωπος 'become human' (GkWaC frequency: 1.9 per million) which has the meaning of "becoming an ethical and useful citizen", thus implying a shift towards a stronger negative judgement about the social attitude of black people.

(23)   **[EN]** We'll let the *niggers, kikes and spics* grab for their piece of the pie.

   [ES] Dejemos que *negros y latinos* se lleven su parte.

   [Back translation] Let the *blacks* and the *Latinos* get their part.

   The leader of the skinhead gang, a middle-aged male, tries to convince Derek that their organisation is going to stop being a small gang and will now grow into something very serious and powerful all over the country. He explains how he plans to act in order to achieve it.

In example (23) above, we mark the use of three racial slurs, *nigger* (enTen-Ten12 frequency: 0.9 per million) as highly negative appreciations towards Jews, Latinos, and black people respectively. In the Spanish TT, the racial slurs of the original are shifted towards neutralisation (*negros* and *latinos*), while the reference to Jews (*kikes*) is eliminated. In all, the negative appreciations that are inherent in racial slurs are eliminated. Although in Spanish there is a lexeme, *negrata*, which has the same derogatory connotation as *nigger*, translating *nigger* as *negro* is a recurrent practice in our corpus. However, *negrata* is a term with a very low frequency (only 97 tokens in esTenTen11), while *nigger* appears with a frequency of 0.9 per million in enTenTen12. This observation could be indicative of the reasons that made Spanish subtitlers opt for the neutral term, avoiding the use of an uncommon term. On the other hand, *spic*, a term that could have been translated as *sudaca* (a Spanish racial slur with presumably similar connotations with 431 tokens in esTenTen11) is also avoided. In both cases, the translator opts for neutralising the rendition of the original utterance.

(24)   [EN] Name your price, *cracker.*

[ES] Di tu precio, *blanco.*

[Back translation] Name your price, white guy.

[EL] Πες το ποσόν, *βλάχο.*

[Back translation] Name your price, country bumpkin.

During a basketball game in the neighbourhood court, members of the skin-head gang start to quarrel with members of a "black gang". Derek has a bet; he proposes a "whites against blacks" game. The answer in (24) comes from one of the opponents, indicating that they accept the bet. In example (24) above, the disparaging term *cracker* (showing negative appreciation, i.e. for a poor white person, usually from the South) is translated as *blanco* 'white' in Spanish, but as *βλάχο* 'country bumpkin' in Greek. In this case, the Spanish subtitler succeeds in maintaining the racial nuance of the term, although the strength of the negative appreciation is diminished, while the Greek subtitler eliminates the racial reference and only transfers the aggressive tone of the dialogue.

(25)   [EN] - Do you speak English? - I am speaking English, you stupid cow!

[EL] - Θα μιλήσετε Αγγλικά; - Μιλάω Αγγλικά!

[Back translation] - Are you going to speak English? - I speak English!

In example (25) above, an Asian woman enters a hospital screaming the name of her husband. The intuitive reaction of the nurse is to ask her if she speaks English, a reaction reflecting the stereotype that immigrants do not speak the language of the host country. Thus, we mark this instance as a low strength negative appreciation, yet expressed in a polite manner. The Greek subtitler opts for a more aggressive-impolite way in rendering this question, *θα μιλήσετε Αγγλικά* 'Are you going to speak English?' strengthening the negative valence of the utterance. There are many similar examples in our corpus, pointing to the linguistic identity as a marker of difference. Sella-Mazi (2001: 111) argues that language is involved in matters of political and social texture, by functioning as the defining element of the nature of multiple human groupings, either positively by delineating "Us", or negatively, by excluding allophones from the said group: in this case, the interlocutors are self-determined contrastingly, both within and outside a linguistic group (the "Others").

(26)   [EN] Stupid *wetback*

         [ES] Estúpida *sin papeles*

         [Back translation] Stupid undocumented immigrant

In (26), an Asian and a Latin American woman are involved in a car crash. While they quarrel, the first one calls the other a *wetback*. The term is highly disparaging and refers to illegal Latin Americans (especially Mexicans) as a descriptor of the way Mexicans enter the US by crossing the Rio Grande. Therefore, it has been marked as a negative judgement utterance. Although the term is decades-old and has been used even in the title of a deportation programme of the US in 1954 (the so-called "Operation Wetback", see Hernandez 2006), today it is used in a highly derogatory manner as a racial slur. As shown in Figure 6, the most significant collocations of wetback (sorted by Mutual-Information, in a query window of -10 to +10 tokens) are other racial slurs, especially in their context of usage (e.g. *mojado, beaners, spics, kike, nigger, chink, greaser, lowlife,* etc.).

On the other hand, the Spanish translation uses *sin papeles* 'undocumented immigrants'. This is a rather neutral term to refer to illegal immigrants. In esTen-Ten11, the most significant collocates of *sin papeles* (see Figure 7) are emotionally neutral (*inmigrante* 'immigrants', *empadronar/empadronamiento* 'inclusion in the town registry', *redadas* 'raids', *patera/pateras* 'dinghy') and an analysis of the concordances shows that the term is used also in texts, in support of the human rights of immigrants.

Collocation candidates

Page 1   Go   Next >

	Freq	MI
P	N mojado	5	21.548
P	N Wetback	6	19.708
P	N wetback	28	19.418
P	N beaners	6	19.200
P	N spics	6	18.866
P	N kike	7	17.176
P	N Belling	6	17.057
P	N Chink	3	17.027
P	N nigger	68	16.606
P	N spic	5	16.273
P	N greaser	3	15.815
P	N lowlife	5	15.319
P	N OPERATION	3	15.083
P	N coon	6	14.741
P	N Boilers	3	14.629
P	N chink	7	14.472
P	N carload	3	14.448
P	N whitey	3	14.371
P	N Operation	73	14.253

Figure 6: Collocates of *wetback* in enTenTen12, sorted by Mutual Information (MI) in SketchEngine

Collocation candidates

Page 1   Go   Next >

	Freq	logDice
P	N empadronar	33	8.094
P	N inmigrantes	724	8.038
P	N inmigrante	122	7.486
P	N ▓▓▓▓	21	7.219
P	N empadronamiento	30	7.018
P	N pateras	21	6.908
P	N patera	21	6.731
P	N emigrantes	53	6.714
P	N Clandestino	12	6.658
P	N Vic	28	6.633
P	N regularización	26	6.451
P	N expulsiones	16	6.362
P	N deportación	12	6.342
P	N regularizar	16	6.291
P	N repatriados	10	6.221
P	N emigrante	15	6.148

Figure 7: Collocates of *sin papeles* in esTenTen11, sorted by logDice in SketchEngine

In other words, the racist tone of the insult, even though it is still present in the Spanish text, is reduced in the interpersonal component of the utterance.

(27)   [EN] - You wanna buy these Chinamen? - Don't be ignorant. They're Thai or Cambodian. Entirely different kind of *chinks*.

         [ES] - ¿Vas a comprar esos chinos? - No seas ignorante. Serán tailandeses o camboyanos. Son unos *amarillos* distintos.

         [Back translation] Should be Thai or Cambodian. They are different yellow people.

Once again, a character of *Crash* uses a racial slur to refer to a group of Asians. He, quite ironically, has just decided to set them free instead of accepting money to "sell" them with the truck he robbed and proved to have been used for human trafficking. This is a negative appreciation texteme. Once again, *chink* (queried in SketchEngine as a noun) was found to collocate with other racial slurs in our reference corpus. However, a similar query for *amarillo* 'yellow' does not yield any results, since as a noun it refers also to the colour, and in the tool used, semantic disambiguation is not possible. However, the use of a colour to designate a race does not necessarily indicate a racist stance, given that the utterance is not directed at Asians. This explanation is consistent with the definition of *amarillo*, taken from the online version of the *Diccionario de la Real Academia Española* (*DRAE*), which is not marked as derogatory, but as simply referring to the Asian race.[21]

5.2 Summary of findings

Each language/culture produces and stabilises forms of expressing (racist) meanings that are unknown or at least asymmetrically[22] represented in other languages and cultures. Racial slurs are a clear example of this and constitute crucial points for the translator, who often mitigates or omits them. Even though the mitigation of racial slurs is the general tendency in our corpus, there are also cases of over-toning of racist attitudes, e.g. in examples (22) and (25); in both these examples, the (racist-oriented) interpersonal meaning is intensified in the TL, though both target utterances lack marked epithets (slurs). Such instances should be explored further. This article has discussed different types of register

---

[21] "Dicho de un individuo o de la raza a que pertenece: De piel amarillenta y ojos oblicuos. Apl. a pers., u.t.c.s." http://goo.gl/oelvVZ.

[22] For a discussion on cultural asymmetry in translation, a concept coined in TS by Even-Zohar (2005), see e.g. Klaudy et al. (2012).

shifts, without attempting to provide a systematic analysis (for instance, we did not consider the many instances of racist discourse which did not undergo significant register shift in translation). Such a systematic analysis, which shall be pursued in further research, will hopefully provide a more "sustainable" picture of how racist discourse is handled in translation.

6 Conclusions

This paper has presented a research, based on the PhD thesis of the first author, aimed at investigating the translation of racist discourse in Anglophone films subtitled in Greek and Spanish.

To this end, we have developed a linguistic annotation model in order to systematically categorise racism-related utterances in original films and in their subtitled versions. Instances of stereotyped views, prejudices, racist attitudes and emotions triggered by racism were coded using an annotation scheme based on Appraisal Theory.

The reference corpora used for the analysis were extremely useful, though with some limitations. Firstly, they were neither corpora of spoken discourse nor balanced corpora. Secondly, some of the terms looked up have very low frequencies and therefore do not allow for a safe description. Thirdly, it was not possible to find reliable evidence for ambiguous terms such as *amarillo* or *sin papeles*. In many cases the meaning of a racist expression could be interpreted only by analysing its context in the film.

Our analysis of register shifts in translation, based on a Systemic Functional Linguistic approach, is promising for the descriptive study of the socio-culturally marked discourse of racism and aims to serve as an explanatory basis for addressing broader questions:

- Is it possible, and if so how, to refine the definitions of heterophobia that have formed part of our initial motivation in functional linguistic terms?

- Which is the relation between cinema and socio-linguistic reality in the perception of xenophobia?

- What are the implications of such an analysis, in relation to the comprehension of racist discourse and its root causes in the modern Greek and European linguistic and cultural reality?

Last but not least, our findings so far point to the assumption that such an approach could, indeed, be linked systematically to the critical study of the role of translation in the diachronic development of the sociolinguistic dimension of racism.

References

Asher, Nicholas, Farah Benamara & Yvette Yannick Mathieu. 2009. Appraisal of opinion expressions in discourse. *Lingvisticae Investigationes* 32(2). 279–292.

Baker, Paul, Costas Gabrielatos, Majid Khosravinik, Michał Krzyżanowski, Tony McEnery & Ruth Wodak. 2008. A useful methodological synergy? Combining critical discourse analysis and corpus linguistics to examine discourses of refugees and asylum seekers in the UK press. *Discourse and Society* 19(3). 273–306.

Batsalia, Frideriki & Eleni Sella-Mazi. 2010. *Linguistic approach to the theory and didactics of translation.* 2nd edition. Athens: Papazisis.

Brugman, Hennie & Albert Russell. 2004. Annotating multimedia/multi-modal resources with ELAN. In *Proceedings of the forth international conference on language resources and evaluation.* Paris: ELRA.

Chesterman, Andrew. 2008. On explanation. In Anthony Pym, Miriam Shlesinger & Daniel Simeoni (eds.), *Beyond descriptive translation studies*, 363–379. Amsterdam: John Benjamins.

Cunningham, Hamish, Diana Maynard, Kalina Bontcheva & Valentin Tablan. 2002. Gate: A framework and graphical development environment for robust NLP tools and applications. In *Proc. 40th Anniversary Meeting of the Association for Computational Linguistics (ACL'02).* Philadelphia.

Eggins, Suzanne & Diana Slade. 1997. *Analysing casual conversation.* London: Cassell.

Essed, Philomena. 1991. *Understanding everyday racism: An interdisciplinary theory.* London: Sage.

Even-Zohar, Itamar. 2005. Laws of cultural interference. In *Papers in culture research.* http://goo.gl/Fvw4ZM.

Fairclough, Norman. 1985. Critical and descriptive goals in discourse analysis. *Journal of Pragmatics* 9. 739–763.

Fairclough, Norman. 1992. *Discourse and social change.* Cambridge: Polity Press.

Fairclough, Norman. 2003. *Analysing discourse. Textual analysis for social research.* London: Routledge.

Forster, Marc. 2001. *Monster's ball.* Corpus. US: Lions Gate Films.

Fotopoulou, Aggeliki, Marianna Mini, Mavina Pantazara & Argiro Moustaki. 2009. La combinatoire lexicale des noms de sentiments en grec moderne. In Iva Navacova & Agnès Tutin (eds.), *Le lexique des émotions.* Grenoble: ELLUG.

Giddens, Anthony. 2009. *Sociology.* 6th edition. Cambridge: Polity Press.

Gottlieb, Henrik. 1997. *Subtitles, translation & idioms.* Copenhagen: University of Copenhagen.

Gottlieb, Henrik. 2005. Multidimensional translation: Semantics turned semiotics. In *Proceedings EU High Level Scientific Conference Series: Multidimensional Translation (MuTra).* Copenhagen.

Haggis, Paul. 2004. *Crash.* Corpus. US: Lions Gate Films.

Halliday, M. A. K. 1978. *Language as social semiotic.* London: Arnold.

Halliday, Michael Alexander Kirkwood & Ruqaiya Hasan. 1976. *Cohesion in English.* London: Longman.

Halliday, Michael Alexander Kirkwood & Christian Matthiessen. 2014. *Halliday's introduction to functional grammar.* 4th edition. London: Routledge.

Hatim, Basil & Ian Mason. 1997. *The translator as communicator.* London: Routledge.

Hernandez, Kelly Lytle. 2006. The crimes and consequences of illegal immigration: a cross-border examination of Operation Wetback, 1943-1954. *Western Historical Quarterly* 37. 421–444.

Jaffe, Alexandra. 2009. *Stance. Sociolinguistic perspectives.* Oxford: OUP.

Jakobson, Roman. 2012. On linguistic aspects of translation. In Lawrence Venuti (ed.), *The Translation Studies reader,* Third edition. London: Routledge.

Jakubíček, Miloš, Adam Kilgarriff, Vojtěch Kovář, Pavel Rychlý & Vít Suchomel. 2013. The TenTen corpus family. In Andrew Hardie & Robbie Love (eds.), *Corpus linguistics 2013 abstract book.* Lancaster: UCREL.

Johansson, Stig. 2003. Reflections on corpora and their uses in cross-linguistic research. In Federico Zanettin, Silvia Bernardini & Domenic Stewart (eds.), *Corpora in translator education.* Manchester: St. Jerome Publishing.

Kaye, Tony. 1998. *American History X.* New Line Cinema.

Kenny, Dorothy. 1998. Creatures of habit? What translators usually do with words. *Meta* 43(4). 515–523.

Kilgarriff, Adam, Pavel Rychly, Pavel Smrz & David Tugwell. 2004. The SketchEngine. In *Proc EURALEX 2004,* 105–116. Lorient, France.

Klaudy, Kinga, Hannu Kemppanen, Marja Jänis & Alexandra Belikova. 2012. Linguistic and cultural asymmetry in translation from and into minor languages. In Hannu Kemppanen, Marja Jänis & Alexandra Belikova (eds.), *Domestication and foreignization in Translation Studies,* 33–48. Berlin: Frank & Timme.

Kress, Gunther. 2010. *Multimodality: a social semiotic approach to contemporary communication.* London: Routledge.

Lawrence, Duncan. 2002. Racial and cultural issues in counselling training. In Aisha Dupont-Joshua (ed.), *Working inter-culturally in counselling settings*, 88–105. London: Routledge.

Lee, Spike. 1989. *Do the right thing.* Corpus. US: Universal/40 Acres & a Mule Filmworks.

Martin, James Robert. 2000. Beyond exchange: Appraisal systems in English. In Susan Hunston & Geoffrey Thompson (eds.), *Evaluation in text*, 142–175. Oxford: OUP.

Martin, James Robert & Peter R. R. White. 2005. *The language of evaluation: Appraisal in English.* London: Palgrave Macmillan.

Mason, Ian. 2001. Coherence in subtitling: The negotiation of face. In Frederic Chaume & Rosa Agost (eds.), *La traducción en los medios audiovisuales*, 19–31. Castellon: Jaume I University of Castellon.

McEnery, Tony & Andrew Hardie. 2012. *Corpus linguistics: Method, theory and practice.* Cambridge: CUP.

Meadows, Shane. 2006. *This is England.* Corpus. UK: Optimum Home Releasing.

Memmi, Albert. 2000. *Racism.* Minneapolis: University of Minnesota Press.

Mouka, Effie. 2014. Investigating translational norms in socioculturally marked cinematographic discourse. In Jenny Brumme & Sandra Falbe (eds.), *The spoken language in a multimodal context. Description, teaching, translation*, 213–228. Berlin: Frank & Timme.

Mouka, Effie, Voula Giouli, Aggeliki Fotopoulou & Ioannis E. Saridakis. 2012. Opinion and emotion in movies: A modular perspective to annotation. In *Proceedings of the eighth international conference on language resources and evaluation*, 104–109. Paris: ELRA.

Mubenga, Kajingulu Somwe. 2009. Towards a multimodal pragmatic analysis of film discourse in audiovisual translation. *Meta* 54(3). 466–484.

Munday, Jeremy. 2012. *Evaluation in translation: critical points of translator decision-making.* London: Routledge.

Pedersen, Jan. 2011. *Subtitling norms for television: an exploration focusing on extralinguistic cultural references.* Amsterdam: John Benjamins.

Pettit, Zoë. 2005. Translating register, style and tone in dubbing and subtitling. *Journal of Specialised Translation* 4. 49–65.

Reisigl, Martin & Ruth Wodak. 2001. *Discourse and discrimination. Rhetorics of racism and antisemitism.* London: Routledge.

Saridakis, Ioannis E. 2010. *Text corpora and translation: Theory and applications.* Athens: Papazisis.

Schmidt, Thomas. 2011. A TEI-based approach to standardising spoken language transcription. *Journal of the Text Encoding Initiative.*

Sella-Mazi, Eleni. 2001. *Diglossia and society. The greek reality.* Athens: Proskinio.

Sinclair, John. 1996. The search for units of meaning. *Textus* 9(1). 75–106.

Taboada, Maite & Jack Grieve. 2004. Analyzing appraisal automatically. In *AAAI spring symposium on exploring attitude and affect in text.*

Teubert, Wolfgang & Anna Čermáková. 2007. *Corpus linguistics. A short introduction.* London: Continuum.

Toury, Gideon. 2012. *Descriptive translation studies and beyond.* 2nd edition. Amsterdam: John Benjamins.

van Dijk, Teun Adrianus. 1993. *Elite discourse and racism.* Newbury Park: Sage Publications.

van Dijk, Teun Adrianus. 1995. Discourse semantics and ideology. *Discourse and Society* 6(2). 243–289.

van Dijk, Teun Adrianus. 2000a. Ideologies, racism, discourse: Debates on immigration and ethnic issues. In Jessika Ter Wal & Maykel Verkuyten (eds.), *Comparative perspectives on racism*, 91–116. Aldershot: Ashgate.

van Dijk, Teun Adrianus. 2000b. *Ideology and discourse: A multidisciplinary introduction.* Barcelona: Pompeu Fabra University. http://goo.gl/LmpjoQ.

van Dijk, Teun Adrianus. 2000c. Parliamentary debates. In Ruth Wodak & Teun Adrianus van Dijk (eds.), *Racism at the top: Parliamentary discourses on ethnic issues.* Klagenfurt: Drava.

van Dijk, Teun Adrianus. 2002. Discourse and racism. In David Goldberg & John Solomos (eds.), *The Blackwell companion to racial and ethnic studies*, 145–159. Oxford: Blackwell.

van Dijk, Teun Adrianus. 2004. Racist discourse. In Ellis Cashmore (ed.), *Routledge encyclopedia of race and ethnic studies*, 351–355. London: Routledge.

Vasileva, K. 2011. 6.5% of the EU population are foreigners and 9.4% are born abroad. Population and social conditions. *Eurostat statistics in focus* 34. http://goo.gl/SZLQ2Y.

von Wright, Georg Henrik. 1971. *Explanation and understanding.* Ithaca: Cornell University Press.

Whitelaw, Casey, Navendu Garg & Shlomo Argamon. 2005. Using appraisal taxonomies for sentiment analysis. In *Proceedings of the 14th acm international conference on information and knowledge management.* http://goo.gl/qbNIJB.

Zabalbeascoa, Patrick. 2008. The nature of the audiovisual text and its parameters. In Jorge Díaz-Cintas (ed.), *The didactics of Audiovisual Translation*, 21–38. Amsterdam: John Benjamins.

Zanettin, Federico. 2012. *Translation-driven corpora: Corpus resources for descriptive and applied translation studies.* Manchester: St. Jerome Publishing.

Chapter 4

Building a trilingual parallel corpus to analyse literary translations from German into Basque

Naroa Zubillaga, Zuriñe Sanz and Ibon Uribarri

The aim of this paper is to present the steps we undertook to build our multilingual-aligned parallel corpus created to analyse translations from German into Basque and to report initial results. Translation into Basque is a quite complex phenomenon, and this complexity is reflected in the design of the corpus. When carrying out research into literary translations from German into Basque, we deal with direct translations from German into Basque, but also with indirect translations through Spanish versions. In order to observe both texts in the case of direct translations and all three texts for indirect translations, we have created an aligned, parallel, trilingual corpus. We have also created a search engine which is linked to the corpus. This allows for easy queries and obtains results from both direct and indirect translations. The research carried out with the corpora presented in this paper has revealed cases of standardisation and interference. Evidence for both of Toury's (2012) translation laws are identified in direct as well as indirect translation.

1 Introduction

This paper looks at the process of creating a trilingual aligned parallel corpus which takes into account direct translations from German into Basque and indirect translations through Spanish versions. We also provide some examples to illustrate the application of this corpus in our ongoing research on German to Basque translation. Creating a multilingual corpus and using it as a tool in our research projects enables us to conduct a systematic work within Translation Studies. According to Corpas Pastor (2008: 216), in less than a decade all

Naroa Zubillaga, Zuriñe Sanz & Ibon Uribarri. 2014. Building a trilingual parallel corpus to analyse literary translations from German into Basque. In Claudio Fantinuoli & Federico Zanettin (eds.), *New directions in corpus-based translation studies*, 61–81. Berlin: Language Science Press

Translation Studies branches, and mainly the descriptive branch, have benefited from corpus linguistics. Studies that are based on well designed and organised corpora lead to a qualitative and quantitative development of the discipline.

Xiao & Yue (2009) give an overview of CBTS on the Holmes-Toury map (Xiao & Yue 2009: 243). Since our approach is descriptive, we concentrate on the descriptive branch of Translation Studies mentioned above, leaving aside the applied and theoretical fields.

The research line initiated by Baker (1993), which focuses on the product, has generated most work in this area. Baker and her colleagues at the University of Manchester created the Translational English Corpus (TEC) and many studies (e.g. Laviosa 1998; Olohan & Baker 2000; Olohan 2003) made use of this corpus to search for translation universals. Xiao & Yue (2009: 244) even state that "the majority of product-oriented translation studies attempt to uncover evidence to support or reject the so-called translation universal hypothesis". Other scholars, such as Kenny (2001), acknowledge the value of monolingual translational corpora, but they also argue that these kinds of studies would benefit from corpora including source texts: "while monolingual translational corpora have been invaluable in attempts to describe the specific nature of translated text and to pinpoint aspects of the styles of individual translators (and not just original authors), some researchers (Laviosa 1998: 565; Puurtinen 1998: 565) have argued that studies based on them may sometimes need to be supplemented by an analysis of the relevant source texts" (Kenny 2001: 62).

Another research line focuses on the process. These kinds of studies are usually based on parallel corpora which help the researcher compare source and target texts. Utka (2004), for example, based on an English–Lithuanian parallel corpus consisting of original European Community law texts and three draft versions (the first translator's draft, the intermediate version and the final translation) for each source text, reports cases of "normalization, systematic replacement of terminology and influence by the original language" (Xiao & Yue 2009: 246). In reference to the development of such parallel corpora, Ji (2010) mentions that, due to the costs and copyright issues, the most commonly used type of corpora is the "small-scale topic-specific parallel corpora" (Ji 2010: 6) and that "the usefulness of this type of DIY corpus, when studied in conjunction with larger-scale comparable corpora, translational or non-translational, may be maximally extended" (Ji 2010: 6).

A third line of research, corpus based function-oriented descriptive studies, has been rather less explored "possibly because the marriage between corpora and this type of research, just like corpus-based discourse analysis (e.g. Baker 2006), is still in the 'honeymoon' period" (Xiao & Yue 2009: 247).

In our case, as lecturers and researchers in the area of Translation Studies at the University of the Basque Country (UPV–EHU) working within the framework of the research group TRALIMA/ITZULIK, we have set up a corpus-based translation study.[1] As we all teach translation courses (from German into Basque and Spanish), we are aware of the benefits a corpus could have for translation didactics. As researchers, on the other hand, our main goal is to look into how translations have been performed from German into Basque; that is, we want to examine translational behaviour. On the one hand, we compare the source text with the corresponding target text(s) based on a parallel corpus. In that sense, the study is process-oriented.[2] However, on the other hand, this research is also product-oriented, since we focus on the target texts and culture in order to explain certain translational phenomena. For this reason we make use of and refer to already existing Basque monolingual corpora, a field that has attracted the attention of Basque researchers since the 1980s.

The first Basque monolingual corpus was created in 1984, and although there was a considerable hiatus until the next corpus was created (2002), generally speaking, this field has been growing constantly. ETC (EgungoTestuenCorpusa),[3] which was made freely available in 2013, contains 204.9 milliòn words and is the largest Basque monolingual corpus created to date. The Basque Institute of the University of the Basque Country has created a reference corpus balanced in terms of type of texts, proportion of original and translated texts, year of publication, and so on.

However, the use of corpora in the academic field of Basque Translation Studies is very recent. Barambones (2012), who analysed the translation into Basque of audio-visual products for children on Basque public television, did use a corpus, but conducted his study by manually arranging the source and target texts in a chart. Manterola (2011) analysed translations of Basque literary works into other languages, focusing on translations of the Basque writer Bernardo Atxaga. She built a large multilingual digital parallel corpus with 12 original works in Basque and their translations into seven languages. She used WordSmith Tools (Scott 2004) to build and analyse her corpus, but encountered problems while aligning her corpus at sentence level and the result of alignment at paragraph level was quite unsatisfactory.

---

[1] GIC 12_197, IT728–13, UFI 11_06, UPV/EHU.

[2] We are aware of the fact that there are other approaches to study translation process, such as think-aloud protocols (TAPs) or the translog system. However, our aim is to study the process at a textual level using the parallel corpus.

[3] The corpus' website is: http://www.ehu.es/etc/.

2 The Aleuska corpus

Taking both of these precedents into account, and since there was no existing corpus linking the languages we wanted to work with, we had to create our own corpus. The starting point was the Aleuska database, a catalogue of German to Basque translations which was started in 2003 and which has been supplemented in subsequent years by consulting different Basque as well as German bibliographical databases, such as the Index Translationum,[4] the Deutsche Nationalbibliothek[5] or the database for the Network of Basque Public Libraries.[6] We now have a catalogue of approximately 700 entries. In addition to the usual data for each entry of the catalogue, such as the original title, the author, the translator, the year of publication and the publisher, we also tried to indicate whether the translation was direct or indirect. The texts were classified either as direct or indirect translations based on peritextual as well as epitextual information. This is of interim value, as the assumed direct/indirect character or the translation has to be verified through a more detailed analysis of the texts in the corpus. The uncertain nature of the information about translation directness makes it appropriate to adopt the term "assumed translations", a term proposed by Toury (1995) for texts with an ambiguous translation status. Thus, by using the term "assumed direct/indirect translation", we are expanding Toury's concept of "assumed translation" to the mode of translation. For instance, detailed analysis has shown that translations catalogued as direct at macro-level could contain traces of indirectness at micro-level. Since we needed to avoid absolute categories, the concepts of assumed direct/indirect translations proved to be useful. As for creating the corpus, and taking into account that we wanted to compare not only the assumed direct translations but also the indirect translations conducted through a mediating text, we decided to create a trilingual corpus comprising the German source text, the mediating Spanish text (when necessary) and the Basque target text.

The authors of the present article are pursuing independent yet linked research projects, and each has built his/her own subcorpus. However, we work with the same methodology and tools and our aim since the beginning has been to sum up our efforts and build a common corpus, called Aleuska corpus. Now, the corpus consists of three subcorpora, designed around the group members' research projects as described below.

---

[4] http://portal.unesco.org/culture/en/ev.php-URL_ID=7810&URL_DO=DO_TOPIC&URL_SECTION=201.html.
[5] http://www.dnb.de/DE/Home/home_node.html.
[6] http://www.katalogoak.euskadi.net/cgi-bin_q81a/abnetclop/O9406/ID0cbc23a1/NT1?ACC=111&LANG=en-US.

One member of the research group analysed the translation of children's and youth literature from German into Basque, specifically the translation of swearwords and of some German modal particles (Zubillaga 2013). The aim of Zubillaga's work was to analyse the translation of certain features of the informal language in children's and youth literature. Due to the fact that children's literature has a double audience and is directed not only at children but also at parents and adults involved in the education of children, the language is often softened to avoid reception problems. In this sense, O'Sullivan stresses the link between pedagogy and the toning down of offensive language in children's and youth literature: "Besonders deutlich erkennbar sind sprachpädagogische Normen der Zielkultur in der Tilgung von Beleidigungen oder Beschimpfungen" (O'Sullivan 2000: 212).[7] Marcelo Wirnitzer, who analysed the translations of the children's author Christine Nöstlinger from German into Spanish, noticed this same tendency: "una comparación de muchos libros y de sus traducciones nos mostraría cómo los traductores cambian insultos por palabras más suaves o simplemente los eliminan [...]. Todo esto depende por supuesto de las características de cada cultura y de los tabúes existentes e imperantes en cada una de ellas" (Marcelo Wirnitzer 2007: 146).[8] At the same time, German modal particles typically belong to the spoken register and appear mostly in informal texts (Helbig 1988: 12; Prüfer 1995: 16). In the case of Basque, there is no significant study of the translation of informal speech with the exception of Barambones (2012), who, as mentioned before, analysed audio-visual products for children on Basque public television. Barambones analysed the general language model used in the translation of audio-visual products from English and concluded that "children's and teenagers' slang is scarcely used [in the Basque translations], perhaps due to the fact that in practice most of these idiomatic expressions are borrowings from Spanish" (Barambones 2012: 166–167). Taking this background into account, Zubillaga's research strove to delve into the translation of swearwords and various German modal particles into Basque, which form part of the informal speech directed at children and youngsters.

Another member of the group has looked into the translation of phraseological units (PU) in literary texts translated from German into Basque (Sanz 2013). The translation of these polylexemic, relatively stable and, to a greater or lesser extent, idiomatic word combinations has been the research object of many stud-

---

[7] "The laws of language pedagogy in a target culture are especially identifiable in cases of deletion of insults or swearwords" (our translation).

[8] "A comparison of many books and translations would show us how translators change insults for milder words or simply eliminate them [...] All this depends of course on the characteristics of each culture and its prevailing taboos" (our translation).

ies, mainly since the 1970s. Research has been carried out in a variety of language combinations, PU-types and methodologies. Higi-Wydler (1989), for instance, analyses 3.700 PUS extracted from literary texts translated from German into French, whereas Segura (1998) researches on German–Spanish and Spanish–German translations. In terms of PU–types, Ji (2010), for example, examines Chinese four-character expressions translated into Spanish and Van Lawick (2006) concentrates on somatism, which are PUS containing words which refer to body parts. Although the use of corpora in PU research is gathering strength as far as methodology is concerned, many studies, even if they are empirical, still "move within the narrow limits of manual analysis" (Marco 2009: 843).

Finally, the third member of the group has created a subcorpus with German philosophical texts and their translations into Basque (a bilingual corpus of 1.2 million words including 32 texts written by 13 different authors). Although German philosophical texts have been translated into many different languages, this type of text has not created much interest in Translation Studies. Uribarri has also published some works on the censorship of German philosophical texts translated into Spanish and Basque during Franco's dictatorship (Uribarri 2008; 2010). His goal is to continue feeding this subcorpus and to provide some research results soon.

In sum, all three research projects presented in the preceding paragraphs focus on the descriptive comparison of direct and indirect translations; and although each of the projects aim to analyse specific elements in detail, all three take the translation laws proposed by Toury (2012) as theoretical framework, namely the law of standardisation and the law of interference.

3 Standardisation and interference in Basque

Toury characterises the standardisation law with the observation that "in translation, items tend to be selected on a level which is *lower* [emphasis in the original] than the one where textual relations have been established in the source text" (Toury 2012: 305). However, in the Basque context, standardisation in translation is confronted with another norm, the official language planning policy. The creation of a standard language is a recent phenomenon: there are still many people in the Basque Country who do not know Basque, and its use in many areas of life continues to remain marginal. As such, the language is considered to still be in a process of normalisation. Therefore, and especially when it comes to translating informal speech, Basque translators face a complex situation: real Basque informal speech shows strong interference from Spanish on the one hand and Basque local dialects on the other. That causes translators to make frequent use of quite neutral words in comparison with the original text. In summary, although translating into Basque is affected by the corrosive law of standardisation in a manner similar to other translations, translating into Basque is even more conditioned by the constructive drive towards a standard form of the language (Barambones 2012). For instance, in her trilingual subcorpus, Zubillaga has found that insults and cursing are quite regularly euphemised in Basque translation, and the pragmatic function of German modal particles is maintained in just 15% of the cases in Basque translations.

In addition to the law of standardisation, Toury also proposes the law of interference, according to which, "[...] phenomena pertaining to the make-up of the source text tend to force themselves on the translators and be transferred to the target text" (Toury 2012: 310). When Toury speaks of the *law of the interference*, he only seems to consider the direct interference of an original text on its translation, but it would be advisable to also consider other possibilities, such as what we have called indirect interference. In fact, Toury stresses the importance of indirect translations in another section of his work (Toury 1995: 129–146), and we believe that this should also be considered when discussing interference. For example, *Pippi Långstrump*, translated from Swedish into English and then from English into Spanish, might show traces of the intermediate English version as well as the original Swedish text in the final Spanish version. However, we hypothesise that it is not the same to translate *Pippi Långstrump* from English into Spanish as it is to translate the same work from English into Basque. For in this case, the translation is performed by a diglossic translator for a diglossic reader in a diglossic community, using indirect tools, i.e. first dictionaries and manuals, which involve the language combination German–Spanish and then those for the Spanish–Basque combination. In summary, we believe that a special kind of interference may be involved in case of minority languages: namely, the interference of the dominant language, which could be called diglossic interference.

To sum up, the following points can be made with respect to translations into Basque. First, we have found cases of diglossic textual interference, in the sense that the translator almost always utilises a Spanish translation of the text to be translated, upon which he/she can more or less rely. At one end of the scale, some translators may translate directly without resorting to the intermediate translation; at the other end, some translators may use the intermediate translation as the source text of their translation, while ignoring the actual source text. However, in many cases we find a more complex situation where the translator uses the source text and the Spanish text (and possibly also some other intermediate texts) to varying degrees. In such cases we have a complex source text – that is a "compiled" source text – which may comprise several different texts but mainly pivots around the Spanish intermediate text. As stated by Toury (1995: 72), "[h]ypothetically identified relationships may also give rise to the assumption that a target text drew on a text in a language other than the assumed, or on more than one source text in more than one language". Significantly, it is very unusual to refer to compiled sources in the paratexts of translations, so that such complex situations basically remain essentially invisible.

Secondly, one can speak of diglossic instrumental interference, meaning that sources of documentation and tools used for translation may often be intermediate. Many translations from German into Basque were performed when there was no direct German to Basque dictionary available. Now, there is a rather small dictionary which, however, does not cover all of the translators' needs.[9] Pello Zabaleta, until recently one of the few translators, who translated directly from German into Basque, also highlights the complexity of the translation process from German into Basque due to the lack of German–Basque dictionaries: "Alemanetik eta itzultzen dugunok, lehendabizi alemanetik gaztelerarakoa ikusi behar dugu, eta ondoren gazteletik euskararakoa, eta ondoren euskaraz begiratu behar dugu ea konforme dagoen" (Zabaleta & Biguri 1995).[10]

Thirdly, one can also speak of a diglossic cognitive interference, in the sense that (leaving aside the source language) Basque translators are usually diglossic bilinguals of varying degrees, who know and use both the "high" or dominant language (Spanish or French) and the "low" or minority language (Basque). As such, their writing in Basque (the target language) is mediated by Spanish or French (the dominant languages). In such a situation, translators usually activate the dominant language in the translation process and this may be apparent in the final result. In her research on German somatisms translated into Basque, Sanz has traced such interference in her trilingual subcorpus.

The following example illustrates this type of interference. The expression "gastar dinero a manos llenas" in the Spanish bridge version is a close rendering of the German "Geld mit vollen Händen ausgeben". However, the target version does not follow that German phraseological expression but it calques another similar Spanish one, "arrojar, o echar, algo por la ventana", producing an uncom-

---

[9] In 2006 Elena Martínez published a Basque–German / German–Basque dictionary, and a second edition was published in 2010. This more recent version has around 32,400 entries in both directions.

[10] "While translating from German and other foreign languages one has to first consult a German–Spanish, then a Spanish–Basque dictionary and, finally, look at the Basque to check that it is appropriate" (our translation).

mon expression in Basque with traces of Spanish interference. Interestingly, the translation follows the source German text as it includes the clause "esaera den bezala" ("as the saying goes"), when in fact the expression used by the translator is not a saying in the target language (but it is in the intermediate language).

Table 1: Interference in German to Basque translation

German original	Spanish bridge version	Target text
Ich fing an, Geld auszugeben – mit vollen Händen, wie man sagt.	Comencé a gastar dinero a manos llenas, como suele decirse.	Hasi nintzen dirua leihotik botatzen, esaera den bezala
[I started spending money like it was going out of fashion [lit. with full hands], as the saying goes.]	[I started spending money like it was going out of fashion [lit. with full hands], as the saying goes.]	[I started throwing money out of the window, as the saying goes.]

In brief, Basque translators do not live in a bubble. On the contrary, they live in a cultural situation where Basque and Spanish (and in the case of the French Basque Country, French), coexist in a diglossic context. Therefore, translators may choose to consult the translations of the same work into Spanish. Most of the tools and documentation they use for translating are written in Spanish and, in the end, the diglossic situation in the translators' minds may interfere with the translation process. Needless to say, this type of diglossic interference is also very relevant for cognitive translation studies and multilingualism studies.

In order to create corpora for these research projects, all texts had to be digitised, aligned and linked to a search engine. In order to do this, we could have used already existing software, but were not able to find a program that would meet all our requirements. Due to the specific nature of our research project, we needed a tool that would suit our needs, and the development of that tool has been an integral part of our work. Previous experience of colleagues with existing software such as WordSmith Tools and the shortcomings they encountered (while aligning long multilingual texts at sentence level) persuaded us to develop our own tool. The creation of an alignment tool within the TRACE research project (a collaboration between the University of León and the University of the Basque Country) allowed us to work with an IT expert to adapt TRACE–Aligner and develop it for our own needs. We believe this could encourage other researchers to create their own corpora and, if necessary, their own tools. The next two sections provide a summary of the corpus building process, followed by a brief preliminary analysis of corpus data.

4 Corpus design

As our aim was to conduct a descriptive analysis, we drew on the methodological recommendations for descriptive translation research set out by Lambert & Van Gorp (1985) from the outset. Before we began to analyse the selected texts at macro- and micro-level, we first studied the preliminary data; this was done by creating the Aleuska catalogue mentioned in §1. This catalogue is a database of all German books translated into Basque, which shall soon be published in the web page of the TRALIMA/ITZULIK research group.[11]

Once the catalogue was complete, we established the selection criteria for works which were going to be part of the corpus: we selected both assumed direct and indirect translations; we aimed for variety in terms of authors, translators and publishing companies; we also selected translations published from the 1980s onwards, as this was the time when the standard Basque literary system started flourishing. Each member of the group compiled his/her subcorpus, depending on the objectives of each research: Zubillaga's subcorpus consists of German children's literature and its translations (AleuskaHGL), Sanz's subcorpus consists of German narrative texts and their translations (AleuskaPhraseo) and Uribarri's subcorpus consists of German philosophical texts and their translations (AleuskaFilo). As AleuskaPhraseo includes texts of adult as well as texts of children's literature, some texts of children's literature are the same in Aleuska-Phraseo and AleuskaHGL. As the creation of these subcorpora was almost simultaneous, Zubillaga and Sanz teamed up in order to share some of the texts they dealt with individually and thus ended up with a larger subcorpus. As shown in Table 1, AleuskaHGL contains 80 texts: 38 texts corresponding to 19 direct translations (with German and Basque versions) and 42 texts corresponding to 14 indirect translations (with German, Spanish and Basque versions). Aleuska-Phraseo contains 110 texts: 68 texts corresponding to 34 direct translations and 42 texts corresponding to 14 indirect translations. AleuskaFilo contains 66 texts corresponding to 33 direct translations. All in all, the entire corpus contains 222 texts, as some of the texts appear in both corpora.

---

[11] http://www.ehu.es/tralima/catalogos/Aleuska.

Table 2: Number and type of texts in the corpus

	AleuskaHGL	AleuskaPhraseo	AleuskaFilo	Total
Direct translations	$19 \times 2 = 38$	$34 \times 2 = 68$	$33 \times 2 = 66$	$78 \times 2 = 146$
Indirect translations	$14 \times 3 = 42$	$14 \times 3 = 42$	0	$22 \times 3 = 66$
Original authors	18	30	13	
Number of words	1,276,280	3,529,533	1,213,261	5,511,204[a]

[a] As AleuskaHGL and AleuskaPhraseo have some texts in common, the actual total number of words is not the result of the addition between the three subcorpora.

5 Creating the Aleuska corpus

5.1 Obtaining the texts

As far as possible, we tried to obtain the texts in digital form either in PDF or RTF format. Some of the texts were available on the internet (e.g. at the Gutenberg Project website[12]), while for others we asked the publishing companies or even the translators themselves if they could provide us with the texts for academic purposes. By this means we managed to collect some of the texts as PDF files. Wherever a digital version was not available, we scanned and saved the books as RTF files.

5.2 Cleaning the files

Having collected all the texts, we had to convert the PDF and RTF files into TXT files and clean them, i.e., correct the errors. The errors which occurred during the OCR (optical character recognition) process with different texts in the three languages had to be corrected manually. Correcting formatting errors such as multiple spaces or multiple carriage returns is time consuming for the researcher. However, at this point we had the help of a program developed by our computer technician, who created a user-friendly program written in Microsoft Access using Visual Basic. The program automatically carries out all the formatting corrections. Without such a program, the process has to be done manually, using the find and substitute commands. However, other common errors, such as misspellings or separated words at the end of line, must be corrected manually with the help of a spell-checker.

---

[12] http://www.gutenberg.org.

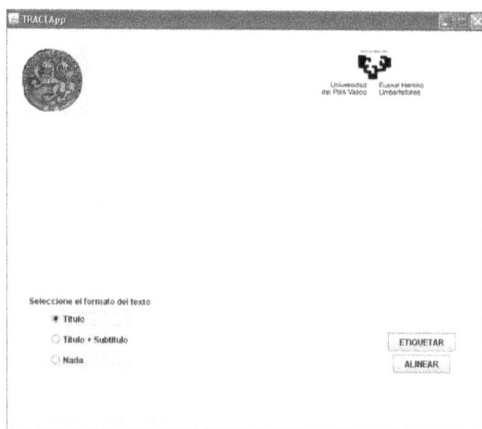

Figure 1: Interface of the tagging/aligning program

After cleaning the texts, it was possible to establish a more detailed description of the contents of the corpus: in total, the aggregate corpus consists of 5,511,204 words, of which 2,722,000 belong to the German source texts, 2,298,472 to the Basque target texts and the rest, 490,732 words, to the intermediary Spanish texts.[13]

5.3 Tagging and aligning with TRACE–Aligner

The third stage involved aligning the texts: this consisted of three steps: tagging the texts, aligning the texts automatically and fine-tuning the alignment manually. Figure 1 shows the interface of TRACE–aligner, the program we developed to create our subcorpora, which gives access to the main functions: tagging (*etiquetar*) and alignment (*alinear*).[14]

Firstly, each text was automatically annotated in XML by automatically adding paragraph and sentence boundaries, to which a header containing metadata (title, author, translator, code, language, translation mode and genre) was added. Providing the texts with metadata becomes essential to subsequently exploit the corpus, as it allows the definition of subcorpora in the queries, i.e. to only search in assumed direct translations, for example, or only in indirect translations. Fig-

---

[13] Since Basque is an agglutinative language, Basque translations usually contain less words than original German texts.

[14] TRACE–aligner is written in Java using Eclipse. We work with an Alpha version (TRACE–aligner 3.0) which we are still testing and developing, but we hope to produce a stable Beta version soon. The "cleaning tool" mentioned above, for instance, is integrated in TRACE–aligner 3.0.

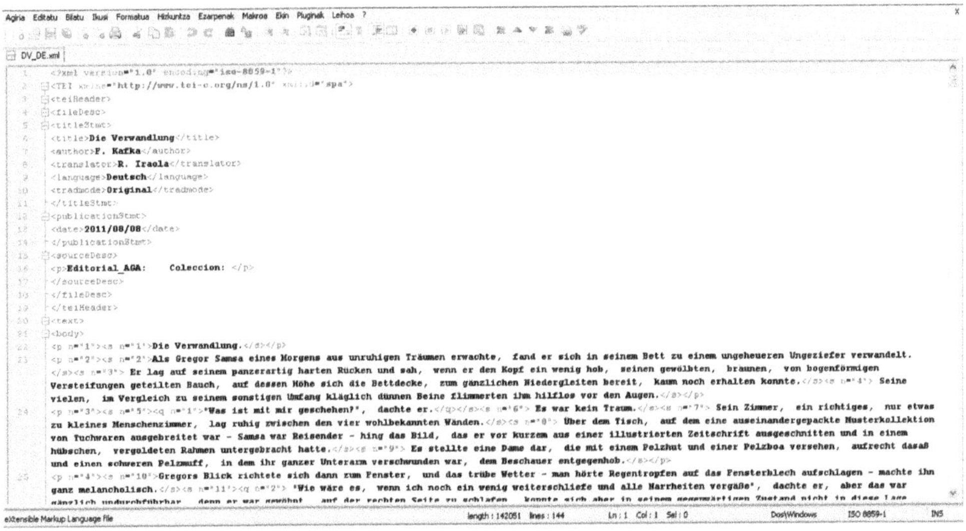

Figure 2: XML annotation of sample text

ure 2 is an example of XML annotation.

Once the texts are annotated, our software tool performs the automatic alignment of the source text and of up to two target texts.[15] That is, the program will automatically align the tagged XML files at the sentence level. The result can be seen in Figure 3. Given that in any translation process one sentence does not necessarily correspond to another, a third step was necessary: the final fine-tuning using manual alignment.

In order to manually edit the results of automatic alignment, we added different editing options to the program, such as "combine", "add cell", "edit" or "split", to make the tool as versatile and as easy to use as possible. The aim during manual alignment editing was to reflect the structure of the original text. This process is absolutely necessary, as different translations of a source text could vary significantly in terms of syntax and sentential structure, and the results displayed by the search engine depend on the alignment modifications made at this stage in accordance with the source text. The outcome of this process is shown in Figure 4.

---

[15] The latest version of the program, TRACE–aligner 3.0, can align multiple texts.

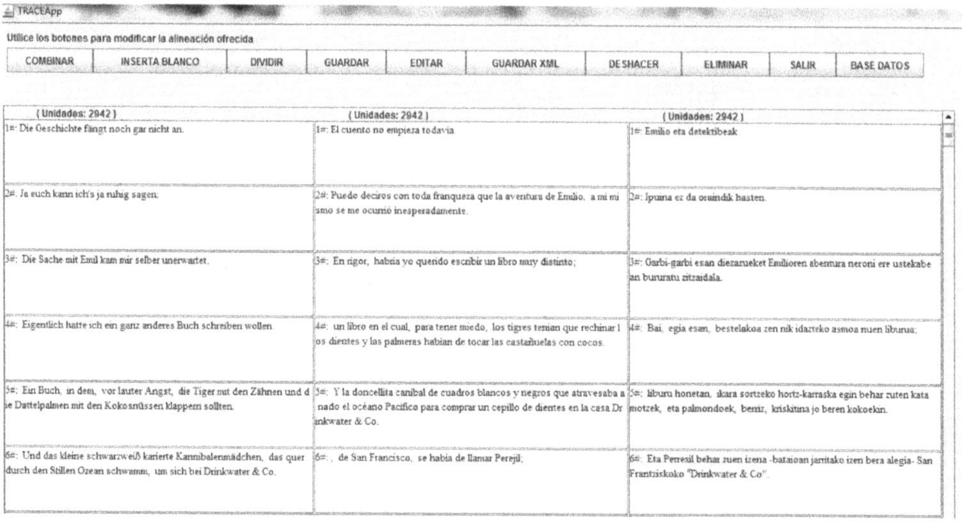

Figure 3: Sample output of automatic alignment

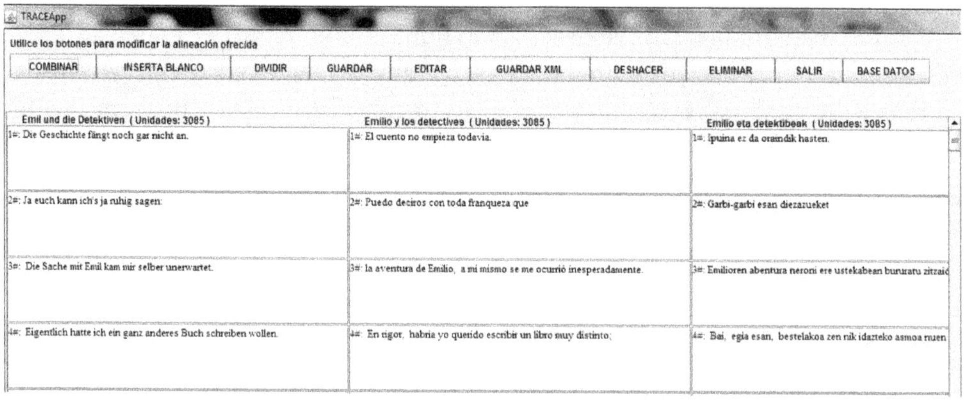

Figure 4: Sample of output after manual alignment editing

5.3.1 Making queries in the database

The tagging/aligning program allows the user to upload the aligned texts into a MySQL database management system (we used the program Xampp for that purpose). Figure 5 shows an image of the database management interface.

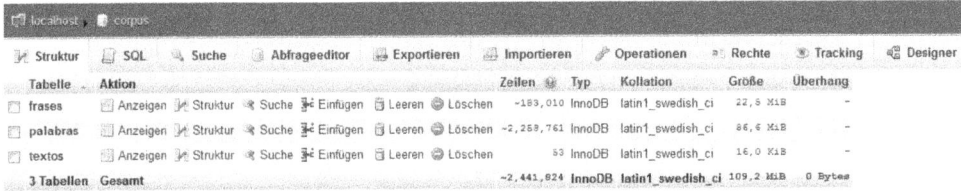

Figure 5: Image of the MySQL database, where the aligned texts are uploaded

Once the aligned texts are uploaded into the database, it is possible to carry out searches using a specifically developed search engine. The inclusion of metadata associated with each text makes it possible to define specific searches: by defining a given language, searches on the source- or the target-text are possible, or the search can be limited to a specific author or translator. As such, different ad hoc subcorpora can be defined with the search criteria. The search engine interface is shown in Figure 6.

Figure 7 shows the results of a search as displayed by the search engine. In this example, the search criteria are German sentences containing the words "Nagel" and "Kopf". The first column contains the code for the aligned texts, the second column the original German text, the third, when applicable, the mediating Spanish texts and the last column the target texts in Basque. Another important feature is that the results are always contextualised: in addition to the sentence containing the words searched for, the preceding and the following sentences are also displayed.

Figure 6: The search engine linked to the database

DEKB	es wurde noch ungemütlicher, denn Trude B. konnte sich nicht verkneifen, den alten Freund, während sie weiterhin in ihrer Kaffeetasse rührte, mit den Worten zu begrüßen "Hallo Herrenbesuch".		oraindik gogorrago izan zen, Trude B. k ezin izan bait zuen isilik gorde, bere kafeari eragiten zion bitartean, adiskide zaharra "kaixo jaun -bisitari" botekin agurtzea.
DEKB	"Ich nehme an", sagte Bloma verlegen, "Trude hat mal wieder den Nagel auf den Kopf getroffen".		- Dirudienez -esan zuen lotsati Blomak-, orain ere Trudek itzeari buru -buruan jo dio.
DEKB	"Ja", sagte Sträubleder, "tragt sich nur, ob das immer taktvoll ist".		- Bai -esan zuen Sträublederrek-, baina ez dakit hori egiaz beti zuzur den.
DKVG	Du wolltest bloß nicht zugeben, daß du um ein Haar abgestürzt wärst!".	¡Tú lo que no querías era admitir que no te has estrellado por un pelo!	Onartu nahi ez zenuena zera zen, txiripaz ez zuzula muturra lurraren kontra apurtu!
DKVG	Daß Anton mit seiner Überlegung den Nagel auf den Kopf getroffen hatte, merkte er an der Reaktion des Vampirs	Por la reacción del vampiro Antón se dio cuenta de que con su observación había dado en el clavo:	Banpiroaren erreakzioaz, Anton bete -betean asmatu zuela ohartu zen:
DKVG	ein verlegenes Grinsen huschte über sein Gesicht.	una tímida sonrisa irónica se deslizó hasta su rostro.	irri barre ironiko tiki bat piztu zitzaion aurpegian.

Figure 7: Example of the results of a search in the corpus

6 Preliminary results

As a result of the process described above, we have created a digital, multilingual and parallel corpus, which is relatively small (over 5 million words) and topic-specific. It may not be a large corpus, but given that it was created according to the criteria which suited our research needs (see §2), it does provide a representative sample of the textual reality we observed. Although the main aim of this article is to describe the process of creating the corpus and the corpus itself,[16] this section presents two examples we have extracted from the corpus and which served as data for our research projects to illustrate how the corpus can be exploited.

A first example comes from Zubillaga's 2013 research on insults in German texts translated into Basque, using the AleuskaHGL subcorpora. In order to search for the most common insults in German, Scheffler's list (2000) was used as a reference. The insults in the list were queried one by one in the search engine and then the results were systematically analysed, paying special attention to cases of standardisation and interference. The following is an example of an indirect translation, that is, the Basque translator never looked at the German, but solely used the Spanish version. The search engine displays the three aligned texts so that we can observe the history of the entire translation process. In this case, the translation was carried out in two separate steps: the work was first translated from German into Spanish, and the Basque translation was conducted three years later, taking the mediating Spanish text as its actual source text. This example, along with various others, was classified as a case of standardisation of an insult.

A *hochnäsige Gans* is somebody who is arrogant or stuck-up. The Spanish version uses the equivalent *ganso orgulloso*, which is a literal translation. *Ganso*

---

[16] We continue to develop TRACE–Aligner and we hope to incorporate text analysis features in the near future (word count, word lists, word frequencies, automatic extraction of collocations and so on).

Table 3: Example of indirect translation

OT	MT	TT
Mein Kind soll keine **hochnäsige Gans** werden (Kästner 1931). [My child won't be an arrogant goose. (meaning: **arrogant**)]	Mi hija no debe convertirse en un **ganso orgulloso** (Kästner 1987). [My daughter won't become an arrogant goose. (meaning: **an arrogant fool**)]	Nire alaba ezin da izan **antzara harroa** (Kästner 1989). [My daughter cannot be an arrogant goose (meaning: **an arrogant goose**, meaning literally the animal)]

is an insult in Spanish, but actually has the meaning of somebody foolish, not arrogant, although that is compensated with *orgulloso*, which means arrogant. The Basque version departs from the Spanish version and also gives the literal translation of the Spanish version, i.e. the dictionary equivalent: *antzara harroa*, but *antzara* 'goose/Gans' has no insulting connotation in Basque, it just has the literal meaning for that type of animal. The final Basque target text is, therefore, standardised, since we understand that the toning down of the offensive language reveals the standardisation of the same. In this example, the insult is completely lost compared to the mediating Spanish text, and we were able to observe that the meaning of the insult in the Spanish version is somewhat modified compared to the original German text. In summary, the literal translation from German into Spanish modifies the meaning, as *Gans* and *ganso* have different connotations in German and Spanish; and the literal translation of the Spanish version into Basque normalises the special meaning attached to *ganso*, since *antzara* has no association with foolish behaviour as is the case in Spanish, nor does it have any relation to arrogance as in German.

Example 2 arose from the AleuskaPhraseo subcorpora, as Sanz (2014) was conducting her analysis on German Phraseology translated into Basque. The example is from an assumed direct translation; that is, the text had supposedly been translated directly from the German original version, and so we digitised and aligned just the German and the Basque versions.[17] This is an example of what

---

[17] Until now, Spanish translations were included in the corpus only when the original texts had been translated through a mediating text. During our research, we realised that it would be very interesting to have the opportunity to consult the Spanish translation in all cases, also when translations were presumably made from the German original, in order to check if there

Table 4: Example of a diglossic interference

German original	Spanish bridge version
Kann jedem mal passieren, daß **ihm die Hand ausrutscht**, wenn er in Rasche ist". (Döblin 1929). [It can happen to anyone that, when he/she gets angry, his/her hand slips (meaning: someone gives another person a slap in the face)]	Edonori gertatzen zaiok, amorrazita dagoenean **eskuak alde egitea**". (Döblin 2000). [It can happen to anyone that, when he/she gets angry, his/her hand runs away]

we called diglossic interference or interference of the dominant language (Spanish, in this case), as described above.

As we can see in the German version, the author uses the German idiom *jmdm rutscht die Hand aus* which – according to Duden 11, a German monolingual dictionary specialised in German idioms and proverbs – has the following meaning "jmd. gibt jmdm. eine Ohrfeige". In other words, the actual meaning of the PU is to give someone a slap in the face, and word for word it can be translated as "someone's hand slips". In the Basque translation, we do not find a PU. We were not able to find the expression used in the Basque version in any dictionary and when we searched for this word combination ("eskuak alde egin") in the large corpora mentioned in §1 (ETC corpus), we found no occurrences. We believe that the translator has made a literal translation of a Spanish PU, which is "escapársele a alguien la mano",[18] because the Basque version is a "word for word" translation. We cannot explain the process of this translation without taking into account that the translator of this text is a diglossic translator, living in a diglossic community, using indirect tools to translate (i.e. German–Spanish dictionaries first, and Spanish–Basque dictionaries afterwards).[19] For these reasons, we consider this to be a case of diglossic interference.

The two cases presented above have shown how we have used the search tool in order to retrieve data from the corpus on the one hand and, on the other, how translation behaviour has been analysed in the framework of our research

---

is any relationship between the Spanish and Basque texts. Therefore, the systematic inclusion of the Spanish translations in the corpus is something we intend to do in the future.

[18] According to María Moliner, a well-known Spanish monolingual dictionary, it means "no poder contenerse de hacer cierta cosa" or not to be able to stop oneself from doing something.

[19] No German–Basque dictionaries existed at the time of the translation in question.

projects. Table 3, in the context of an indirect translation process, shows a case of toning down, which we link with the law of standardisation. Table 4 represents a case of interference which, however, does not stem from the German source text but rather from the translator diglossic competence. In this and other cases, although the translation was nominally direct from German, the Basque target texts contained interferences from another language, Spanish in our case.

7 Conclusions

The aim of this article was to explain and present the steps we undertook to build up our corpora and to report initial results. Thanks to the teamwork with our computer technician, we were able to create a user-friendly program and with its help we can now build up our own digitalised, aligned and searchable multilingual corpora.

On the technical side, we are developing TRACE–Aligner 3.0. The updated and improved version can now align more than 3 texts and the database production is much simpler. We will next integrate some text analysis features, starting with those present in model tools like AntConc[20] and WordSmith Tools. We are also working on the integration of all three existing subcorpora into one general German to Basque parallel corpus consisting of over 5 million words, which will be soon locally available for internal use among researchers of our faculty. The publication of the entire corpus or parts thereof is under consideration, but this move is hindered by copyright issues.

In the matter of use and exploitation, our work is at an early stage; however, we were able to identify both standardisation and interference at work in a context, where the development of a standard form of Basque is an additional factor. Our initial results (for example, regarding different types of interference) now need to be checked with further studies. On the other hand, the process of creating our corpus is a long-term investment which can have many different applications in the future. It can be the departing point for further empirical and systematic research on German to Basque translations and may also play a role in translation didactics, lexicography, contrastive linguistics and other related areas. Our corpus could also serve as a model for similar work with translations from other source languages into Basque and, in the process, could help broaden the picture to the larger field of translations into Basque.

---

[20] http://www.laurenceanthony.net/antconc_index.html.

Acknowledgements

We would like to thank our computer technician, Iñaki Albisua, who has developed TRACE–Aligner 2.0 and TRACE–Aligner 3.0.

References

Baker, Mona. 1993. Corpus linguistics and translation studies: Implications and applications. In Mona Baker, Gill Francis & Elena Tognini-Bonelli (eds.), *Text and technology: In honour of John Sinclair*, 233–250. Amsterdam: John Benjamins.

Baker, Paul. 2006. *Using corpora in discourse analysis.* London: Continuum.

Barambones, Josu. 2012. *Mapping the dubbing scene: Audiovisual translation in Basque television.* Frankfurt am Main: Peter Lang.

Corpas Pastor, Gloria. 2008. *Investigar con corpus en traducción: Los retos de un nuevo paradigma.* Frankfurt am Main: Peter Lang.

Helbig, Gerhard. 1988. *Lexikon deutscher Partikeln.* Leipzig: VEB, Verlag Enzyklopädie Leipzig.

Higi-Wydler, Melanie. 1989. *Zur Übersetzung von Idiomen: eine Beschreibung und Klassifizierung deutscher Idiome und ihrer französischen Entsprechungen.* Frankfurt am Main: Peter Lang.

Ji, Meng. 2010. *Phraseology in corpus-based translation studies.* Frankfurt am Main: Peter Lang.

Kenny, Dorothy. 2001. *Lexis and creativity in translation.* Manchester: St. Jerome Publishing.

Lambert, José & Hendrik Van Gorp. 1985. On describing translations. In Theo Hermans (ed.), *The manipulation of literature: Studies in Literary Translation.* London: Croom Helm.

Laviosa, Sara. 1998. Core patterns of lexical use in a comparable corpus of English narrative prose. *Meta: Translators' Journal* 43. 557–570.

Manterola, Elizabete. 2011. *Euskal literatura beste hizkuntza batzuetara itzulia: Bernardo Atxagaren lanen itzulpen moten arteko alderaketa* PhD thesis.

Marcelo Wirnitzer, Gisela. 2007. *Traducción de las referencias culturales en la literatura infantil y juvenil.* Frankfurt am Main: Peter Lang.

Marco, Josep. 2009. Normalisation and the translation of phraseology in the COVALT Corpus. *Meta* 54(4). 842–856.

Olohan, Maeve. 2003. How frequent are the contractions? A study of contracted form in the translational english corpus. *Target* 15. 59–89.

Olohan, Maeve & Mona Baker. 2000. Reporting that in translated english: Evidence of subconscious processes of explicitation. *Across Languages and Cultures* 2(1). 141–158.

O'Sullivan, Emer. 2000. *Kinderliterarische Komparatistik*. Mörlenbach: Universitätsverlag C. Winter Heidelberg.

Prüfer, Irene. 1995. *La traducción de las partículas modales del alemán al español y al inglés*. Frankfurt am Main: Peter Lang.

Puurtinen, Tiina. 1998. Syntax, readability and ideology in children's literature. *Meta* 43. 524–533.

Sanz, Zuriñe. 2013. Korpusbasierte Übersetzungsanalyse von Hand-Somatismen (Deutsch-Baskisch). In Melanija Fabčič, Sabine Fiedler & Joanna Szerszunowicz (eds.), *Phraseologie im interlingualen und interkulturellen Kontakt*, 317–330. Maribor: Zora.

Sanz, Zuriñe. 2014. *The translation of phraseological units: German-Basque. A corpus-based study* PhD thesis.

Scott, Mike. 2004. *Wordsmith Tools*. Liverpool: Lexical Analysis Software.

Segura, Blanca. 1998. *Kontrastive Idiomatik, Deutsch-Spanisch: eine textuelle Untersuchung von Idiomen anhand literarischer Werke und ihrer Übersetzungsprobleme*. Frankfurt am Main: Peter Lang.

Toury, Gideon. 1995. *Descriptive translation studies and beyond*. Amsterdam: John Benjamins.

Toury, Gideon. 2012. *Descriptive translation studies and beyond*. 2nd edition. Amsterdam: John Benjamins.

Uribarri, Ibon. 2008. Translations of German philosophy and censorship. In Teresa Seruya & Maria Lin Moniz (eds.), *Translation and censorship in different times and landscapes*, 103–118. Newcastle: Cambridge Scholars Publishing.

Uribarri, Ibon. 2010. German philosophy in nineteenth century Spain: Reception, translation and censorship in the case of Immanuel Kant. In Denise Merkle, Carol O'Sullivan, Luc Van Doorslaer & Michaela Wolf (eds.), *The power of the pen. Translation and censorship in nineteenth century Europe*, 77–95. Vienna: LIT Verlag.

Utka, Andrius. 2004. Phases of translation corpus: Compilation and analysis. *International journal of corpus linguistics* 9(2). 195–224.

Van Lawick, Heike. 2006. *Metàfora, fraseologia i traducció. Aplicació als somatismes en una obra de Bertolt Brecht*. Aachen: Shaker.

Xiao, Richard & Ming Yue. 2009. Using corpora in translation studies: The state of the art. In Paul Baker (ed.), *Contemporary Corpus Linguistics*, 237–261. London: Continuum.

Zabaleta, Patrick & Koldo Biguri. 1995. Pello Zabaletarekin solasean. *Senez* 10. http://www.eizie.org/Argitalpenak/Senez/19901131/pello[30/03/2013].

Zubillaga, Naroa. 2013. *Alemanetik euskaratutako haur-eta gazte-literatura: Zuzeneko nahiz zeharkako itzulpenen azterketa corpus baten bidez* PhD thesis. http://www.ehu.es/argitalpenak/images/stories/tesis/Humanidades/8670ZubillagaEU.pdf.

Chapter 5

Variation in translation: Evidence from corpora

Ekaterina Lapshinova-Koltunski

The present paper describes a corpus-based approach to study variation in translation in terms of translation features. We compare texts, which differ in the source/target texts (English vs. German), production types (original vs. translation) and method of translation (human, computer-aided = CAT, machine) in terms of a theoretically-motivated set of features. In this study, we decide for the features which can be easily obtained on the basis of automatic corpus annotations, i.e. tokens, lemmas and part-of-speech tags. Our results show that there is variation in the mentioned translations in terms of the features under analysis.

1 Introduction: Aims and Motivation

In this paper, we apply corpus-based methods to analyse translation variants – translations from English into German produced with different translation methods.

Although numerous studies on translation operate with corpus-based methods, most of them concentrate on the questions concerning the nature of translations and their specific features, (e.g. Baker 1993; 1995; Laviosa 2002; Chesterman 2004) and others. The majority of them tried to generalise translation by defining certain rules or regularities of translated texts. Moreover, they mostly compare translations with originals, i.e. differences or similarities between translations and their source texts or comparable non-translated texts, ignoring variation which can be observed in different translation variants. Corpus-based studies dedicated to the analysis of variation phenomena involving translations, (e.g. Teich 2003; Steiner 2004; Neumann 2013), etc. concentrate on the analysis of human translations only. However, nowadays, translations are produced not only

Ekaterina Lapshinova-Koltunski. 2014. Variation in translation: evidence from corpora. In Claudio Fantinuoli & Federico Zanettin (eds.), *New directions in corpus-based translation studies*, 81–99. Berlin: Language Science Press by humans but also with machine translation (MT) systems. Furthermore, new variants of translation appear due to the interaction of both, e.g. in computer-aided translation or post-editing.

In some works on machine translation the focus lies on comparing different translation variants, such as human vs. machine, as in (White 1994; Papineni et al. 2002; Babych & Hartley 2004; Popovic 2011). However, they all serve the task of automatic MT system evaluation and use the human-produced translations as references or training material only. None of them provide an analysis of specific linguistically motivated features of different text types translated with different translation methods, which is the aim of the present analysis.

In this study, we aim to apply corpus-based methods to prove the knowledge of translation features on a new dataset which contains different variants of translations, including human and machine translation.

The remainder of the paper is structured as follows. §2 presents studies we adopt as theoretical background for the selection of features under analysis. In §3.1, we describe the resources and methods used. In §4, we present the results of our analyses and their discussion, and in §5, we draw some conclusions and provide more ideas for future work.

2 Theoretical Background

Since the present study concentrates on the analysis of linguistic features of different translation variants, we address the existing studies on translation for their definition.

2.1 Related Feature Work

As already mentioned in §1 above, in most cases, these studies either analyse differences between original texts and translations (House 1997; Matthiessen 2001; Teich 2003; Hansen 2003; Steiner 2004), or concentrate on the properties of translated texts only (Baker 1995). Nevertheless, an important point is that most of them consider translations to have their own specific properties which distinguish them from the originals: both their source texts and comparable texts in the target language. These features establish the specific language of translations which is called *translationese* (Gellerstam 1986). Comparing Swedish translations from English with Swedish original texts, the author stated significant differences between them, whereas not all of them were attributable to the source language. This coincides with what Frawley (1984) called "third code", describing features of translational language which are supposed to be different from both source and target languages.

Later, Mona Baker emphasised general effects of the process of translation that are independent of source language, e.g. in Baker (1993; 1995). Analysing characteristic patterns of translations, she excluded the influence of the source language on a translation altogether. Within this context, she proposed *translation universals* – linguistic features which typically occur in translated rather than original texts. According to Baker (1993), they are independent of the influence of the specific language pairs involved in the process of translation. Other scholars (e.g. Toury 1995 or Chesterman 2004) operate with other terms – "laws" or "regularities". We prefer to use the term "translation features" or "phenomena" in the present study: to claim the features "universal" we would need to analyse more language pairs and translation directions, and to call them "laws" and "regularities", we would need to test more conditions, e.g. cognitive factors, status of translation, etc., which is not possible with the bilingual dataset at hand.

Translation features can be classified according to different parameters. For instance, Chesterman (2004) makes a distinction between *S-universals* and *T-universals*: the first comprises differences between translations and their source texts, and the second covers the differences between translations and comparable non-translated texts. A more fine-grained classification includes the following features: *explicitation* – tendency to spell things out rather than leave them implicit, *simplification* – tendency to simplify the language used in translation, *normalisation* – a tendency to exaggerate features of the target language and to conform to its typical patterns, *levelling out*– individual translated texts are more alike than individual original texts, in both source and target languages, and *interference* – features of the source texts are observed in translations. For the second last, we prefer the term convergence proposed by Laviosa (2002), which implies a relatively higher level of homogeneity of translated texts with regard to their own scores on given measures of universal features, e.g. lexical density, sentence length, etc. in contrast to originals. For the last feature, we also prefer to use the term *shining through* defined by Teich (2003).

All these features have been widely analysed in corpus-based translation studies for different language pairs, e.g. in Laviosa (1996) for English translations from a variety of source languages, in Mauranen (2000) for English–Finnish translations, in Teich (2003) for English and German translations, and others. Yet, all of them concentrate on human translations only.

Moreover, some recent corpus-based studies applied machine learning supervised methods to automatically differentiate between translations and originals (e.g. Baroni & Bernardini 2006). These approaches found application in some recent works on natural language processing, e.g. those on cleaning parallel corpora obtained from the Web, or improvement of translation and language models in MT (e.g. Kurokawa, Goutte & Isabelle 2009; Koppel & Ordan 2011; Lembersky, Ordan & Wintner 2012).

We employ the knowledge from these studies, as well as techniques applied to explore the differences between translation variants under analysis, including the features related to their source texts as well as those of comparable target texts.

2.2 Translation Features and their Operationalisation

We group the features described above into three classes according to their correlations, especially in their operationalisation: 1) *simplification,* 2) *explicitation,* 3) *normalisation* vs. *shining through* and 4) *convergence.* Simplification can be analysed on different levels, e.g. lexical, syntactic or semantic. If core patterns of lexical use are observed (see Laviosa 1998), we can identify simplification comparing the proportion of content vs. grammatical words. Translated texts have a relatively low percentage of content words, and the most frequent words are repeated more often. This means, that both lexical density and type–token–ratio of translations are lower than those of their source texts and the comparable texts in the target language. Besides, more general terms are expected to be used in translations. On the level of syntax, one can observe short sentences which replace long ones and a lower average sentence length in general.

Explicitation involves the addition and specification of lexical and grammatical items, with the help of which implicit information in the source text is "spelled out" in its translation. The indicators of this feature include a higher ratio of function words which make grammatical relations explicit, specific terms replacing more general terms (the opposite of simplification), disambiguation of pronouns, increased use of cohesive devices, e.g. conjunctions, and others. In terms of cohesion, one would also expect more nominal (expressed with nominal phrases) than pronominal reference (expressed with personal pronouns) in translations.

Simplification and explicitation features correlate and may be just the opposite of each other. For example, if we observe more specific terms replacing general terms in translation, we face the feature of explicitation, and not simplification. Normalisation and "shining through" can also be measured on different levels, depending on the languages involved. Both features depend on the contrasts between these languages: normalisation implies the exaggerated use of the patterns typical for the target languages, whereas "shining through" involves the patterns typical for the source language (but not specific for the target language) that can be observed in translations. For instance, normalisation can be verified by a great number of typical collocations and neutralised metaphoric expressions. Baker (1996) claims that influence of normalisation depends on the status of the source language: "the higher the status of the source text and language, the less the tendency to normalise". We assume that the languages with a higher status also tend to "shine through" more often. For example, if we analyse translations from English, we would probably observe more "shining through" than normalisation, as English has the highest world language status.

And finally, convergence is a homogeneity feature of translations: they reveal less variation if we compare them to original texts. Convergence can also be observed on all levels of a language system. In accordance with the convergence phenomenon, one would expect that the lexical, grammatical and syntactic features under analysis will reveal smaller differences in translations than in originals.

2.3 Hypotheses

For our analysis of translation variants, we select a set of operationalisation of the features described in §2.2 above.

1. **Simplification** - We expect that our translated texts have a lower percentage of content words vs. grammatical words than their English source texts and the comparable German texts. Also, words are repeated more often in translations. Thus, we observe lower lexical density and type–token–ratio in our translations. In the analysis of English to German translations, we exclude sentence length as operationalisation for simplification. Due to the systemic differences in the morphology, German sentences are generally shorter than those in English, as they contain one-word compounds. To measure this uniformly, we need to split compounds and measure their parts as tokens, which is not feasible within this study.

2. **Explicitation** - Our translated texts reveal more cohesive explicitness than English and German originals: we can observe more conjunctions, less pronominal reference and less general nouns in translations than in English and German originals.

3. **Normalisation/ shining through** - If the translations under analysis demonstrate features more typical for English than for German, we observe "shining through". If there are more features typical for German originals,

then our translations demonstrate normalisation. Here, we use the knowledge from contrastive analysis, e.g. German–English contrasts described in Hawkins (1986), König & Gast (2007), Steiner (2012). For example, we know that English is more "verbal" than German. This can be proved by comparing the distribution of nominal and verbal phrases in both translations and originals. English originals are expected to contain more verbal than nominal phrases. The phenomenon of "shining through" will be confirmed in our data if translations contain more verbal phrases than German originals. On the contrary, if they contain less verbal phrases than German originals, the normalisation hypothesis will be confirmed.

4. **Convergence** - The variation of the features in 1 to 3 is not great if we compare translation variants: they are similar to each other, i.e. the features are distributed homogeneously.

3 Resources, Methods and Tools

To prove the hypotheses formulated in §2.3, we need to compare the distribution of the features under analysis across translation variants, their English sources as well as comparable German originals. For this, we analyse frequency distribution information of lexico-grammatical patterns which serve as operationalisation for these features. The patterns are extracted from a corpus at hand, and evaluated with univariate statistical methods (e.g. significance analysis).

3.1 Corpus Resources

For our investigations, we use VARTRA-SMALL, (see Lapshinova-Koltunski 2013), a translation corpus which contains German translation variants from English produced with different translation methods: by (1) human professionals (PT), (2) human inexperienced translators (CAT), with (3) rule-based MT systems (RBMT) and (4) two statistical MT systems (SMT1 and SMT2). Translations by professionals (PT) were exported from the already existing corpus CroCo (Hansen-Schirra, Neumann & Steiner 2013). The same corpus provides source English texts (EO) and comparable German originals (GO). Thus, we can compare source English texts with their multiple translations into German, as well as to comparable German originals.

The CAT variant was produced by trained translators with at least BA degree, who have no/little experience in translation. All of them applied computer-aided

tools while translating the given texts.[1] The rule-based machine translation variant was translated with SYSTRAN (RBMT),[2] whereas for statistical machine translation we have two further versions – the one produced with Google Translate[3]
(SMT1), and the other – with a self-trained Moses system (SMT2) (see Koehn et al.
2007).

The analysed dataset covers seven registers of written language: political es-
says (ESSAY), fictional texts (FICTION), manuals (INSTR), popular-scientific articles
(POPSCI), "letters to share-holders" (SHARE), prepared political speeches (SPEECH),
and tourism leaflets (TOU). The size of all translation variants in VARTRA-SMALL
comprises approx. 600 thousand tokens. The subcorpora of originals from CroCo
comprise around 250 thousand words each.

All subcorpora under analysis are tokenised, lemmatised and tagged with part-
of-speech information, segmented into syntactic chunks and sentences. The annotations of the VARTRA-SMALL subcorpora were obtained with Tree Tagger (see
Schmid 1994). The availability of these annotation levels in both corpora allows us to analyse certain lexico-grammatical patterns – operationalisation of
the translation features under analysis, defined in §2.3.

The subcorpora are encoded in CWB format (CWB, 2010) and can be queried
with the help of the CQP regular expressions described in Evert (2005).

Alignment on sentence level is available for professional translations only:
each translation is aligned with its English source on sentence level. No alignment is provided for further translation variants at the moment. However, this
annotation level is not necessary for the extraction of the operationalization used
in the present paper.

3.2 Feature Extraction

As already mentioned in §3.1 above, the corpus at hand can be queried with CQP,
which allows the definition of language patterns in form of regular expressions
based on string, part-of-speech and chunk tags as well as further constraints.

To prove the hypothesis for simplification indicated by lexical density (proportion of content words), we extract information on the distribution of content
words in our corpus, for which the query 1 in Table 1 is used.

To extract the corpus evidence of explicitation, we apply queries 2 to 5. Query 2
is used to extract all occurrences of coordinating and subordinating conjunctions,

---

[1] We used the open source tool ACROSS, see www.my-across.net.
[2] SYSTRAN 6.
[3] http://translate.google.com/.

Table 1: Queries for feature extraction

	query element	explanation
1	[pos="vv.*|n.*|adj.*|adv"]	a full verb/noun or an adjective/adverb
2	[pos="kon|kous"]	connector or subordinator
3	<np>[pos="ppe.*"]+</np>	nominal phrase filled with a pronoun
4	<np>[ ]+</np>	any nominal phrase
5	[lemma=re($general)]	nouns from a list
6	(<np>[]+</np>)|(<pp>[]+</pp>)	nominal phrase or prepositional phrase
7	<vp>[]+</vp>	verbal phrase

whereas queries 3 and 4 are used for extraction of information on pronominal vs. nominal reference in the corpus.

We calculate this as proportion of nominal phrases filled with personal pronouns (query 3) to all nominal phrases in the corpus (query 4). Query 5 is used to extract occurrences of general terms in order to compare their proportion to all nouns in the dataset. For this, we use a simple lexical search – we extract a closed class of lexical items of which we know the members. Here, we use lists of general nouns as defined in (Dipper, Seiss & Zinsmeister 2012). For normalisation/shining through, we extract all occurrences of nominal and prepositional phrases (query 6) vs. verbal phrases (query 7). Convergence is proved with the help of all patterns described above.

As we operate with low-level features which do not require formulation of complex lexico-grammatical patterns, we believe that our feature extraction procedures are adequate for the present task. Its only shortcoming is the potential noise caused by tagging errors, especially in case of machine translation. In the latter, we observe a number of untranslated words which are tagged as named entities by automatic part-of-speech taggers. In the longer run, we aim to include deeper structures into our analysis which would require parsed data.

4 Results and their Interpretation

4.1 Simplification

In the first step, we want to test if lexical density and type–token–ratio are lower in translation variant than in eo and go.

Table 2: STTR and LD in VARTRA-SMALL

	EO	GO	PT	CAT	HU-$\bar{x}$	RBMT	SMT1	SMT2	MT-$\bar{x}$	Trans-$\bar{x}$
LD	45.72	45.49	46.23	44.60	45.64	45.08	46.02	47.86	46.30	45.97
STTR	367.5	369.9	360.8	336.4	348.6	335.2	350.4	309.0	331.5	338.4

As already mentioned above, lexical density (LD in Table 2) is measured as a proportion of all content words in our corpus. Unexpectedly, average lexical density in translations (Trans-$\bar{x}$ in Table 2) does not differ from that of both source and comparable originals. Moreover, if we consider the mean values for human and machine translations separately (HU-$\bar{x}$ and MT-$\bar{x}$ respectively); the latter demonstrates even higher LD than human translations and English and German originals. The lowest figure is obtained for CAT, which demonstrates a value below the average. The highest value is observed for SMT2 (47.86).

We explain this by the lexical constraints of the Moses-based system: this system depends on the parallel data used for its training. If the parallel data does not contain translations for some words in a text to be translated, the system keeps them untranslated. In the automatic part-of-speech tagging, these words are then tagged as proper nouns (NE) which leads to their high amount in texts, as seen in example (1).

However, the overall difference between originals and translations is not great, which means that lexical density is not an indicator of simplification in our dataset, as the translated texts show an amount of content words similar to that of the source and comparable originals.

(1) Wenn Sie   strongly , believe , wie   ich , dass Großbritannien
      KOUS PPER NE $ NE $ KOKOM PPER $ KOUS NE
      einen zentralen Platz einnehmen müssen in   Europe's
      ART   ADJA   NN   VVINF   VMINF APPR NE
      decision-making...
      NE

Another indicator of simplification is type–token–ratio which we measure as standardised type–token–ratio (STTR) – a percentage of different lexical word forms (types) per text. As expected, on average, translations show lower STTR than their source texts and comparable originals, see Table 2. Mean value of human translations is also higher than that of machine (348.6 vs. 338.6 respectively). Within translations, the highest STTR, thus, the most lexically rich translation variant in our corpus, is the one produced by professional human translators (360.8), followed by SMT1 (350.4), and CAT (336.4). The level of the latter is close to the average of all translations but lower than that of human translations. The lowest figure is obtained for SMT2 (309.0). This can once again be explained by the fact that this translation variant contains a great deal of untranslated English words, the lemmas of which cannot be identified by the lemmatiser and thus is replaced with "<unknown>", see example (2).

(2) Closing   die Gap   Zwischen *Supply*   und Die Nachfrage
     <unknown> d *<unknown>* zwischen *<unknown>* und d   Nachfrage
     nach A *balanced*   , umfassende Energiepolitik ist   dringend
     nach A *<unknown>* , umfassend Energiepolitik sein dringend
     erforderlich , die langfristige Stärke der amerikanische wirtschaftlichen
     erforderlich , d   langfristig Stärke d   amerikanisch wirtschaftlich
     und nationalen.
     und national *<unknown>*

Interestingly, student translations are closer to the RBMT translation variant in terms of both STTR (336.4 vs. 335.2) and LD (44.60 vs. 45.08). Analysing human and machine translation separately, we observe the same ranking in terms of both indicators: PT > CAT, whereas it is not stable in machine translation: while SMT2 ranks first in LD, it occupies the last position with its STTR value.

4.2 Explicitation

To analyse this feature in our corpus, we measure cohesive explicitness in all subcorpora. Here, we calculate the relative frequencies for conjunctions (conj in Table 3, normalised to the total number of words per thousand), proportion of nominal phrases filled with pro-forms vs. full nominal phrases (pronNP in Table 3, normalised per thousand), as well as proportion of general nouns vs. all noun occurrences (gennoun in Table 3 normalised per thousand) in translations and English and German originals.

According to our hypothesis in §2.3, we expect more conjunctions, less pronominal reference and less general nouns in translations than in originals. If we compare the values of all translations (Trans-$\bar{x}$) with those of their originals, our hypothesis can be confirmed for pronominal reference and general nouns only: Trans-$\bar{x}$ (137.76) < EO (204.67) and Trans-$\bar{x}$ (20.51) < EO (48.71). Translations demonstrate a lower and not higher distribution of conjunctions, Trans-$\bar{x}$ (50.67) < EO (53.80), contrary to what was expected. If we consider human and machine

Table 3: Explicitation indicators

	conj	PRONNP	gennoun
EO	53.80	204.67	48.71
GO	43.58	127.14	23.85
PT	47.58	232.76	19.64
CAT	49.67	139.12	19.93
HU-$\bar{x}$	48.33	184.67	19.74
RBMT	53.32	144.46	23.18
SMT1	52.54	143.15	21.22
SMT2	53.69	39.85	19.46
MT-$\bar{x}$	53.18	107.65	21.19
Trans-$\bar{x}$	50.76	137.76	20.51

translation separately, we see that values for machine translation are much closer to EO (53.18 vs. 53.80), which means that in these translation variants, cohesive relation expressed via conjunctions, were preserved similarly to their English originals. Conversely, fewer conjunctions were used in human translation. The number is still higher than observed in German originals (43.58); therefore, we cannot assume the phenomenon of normalization here. This means that, in our dataset, human translators tend to keep that relation implicit, as seen in example (3).

(3) a. Negative molecules moved into the nurse cells if the egg was made negative, while positive molecules stayed put (EO-POPSCI).

      b. Wenn das Ei auch negativ war, bewegten sich negativ geladene Moleküle in die Nährzellen, positiv geladene Moleküle blieben an Ort und Stelle (PT-POPSCI).

Admittedly, our extractions exclude occurrences of adverbial conjunctions (as we extract coordinating and subordinating conjunctions only). Previous analyses (e.g. Kunz & Lapshinova-Koltunski 2014) show that this syntactic type of conjunction is highly frequent in German. We suppose that English coordinating and subordinating conjunctions are in some cases translated with adverbials in German.

Example (4) extracted from our corpus demonstrates variants of translation of the English subordinating conjunction "while". In both human translations (b.

and c.), conjunctive relation is transferred with an adverbial phrase. In machine translated variants (d. to f.), "while" is translated directly with *während*, so the type of cohesive conjunction is preserved as it was in the original.

(4)   a.   And *while* this will vary from quarter to quarter based on large cash outlays such as tax payments and end-of-year compensation payments, we were pleased with our average positive cash flow for the year from operations of $ 1.5 billion per quarter. (EO-SHARE).

   b.   Dieser Wert schwankt bei Betrachtung verschiedener Quartale. Dafür sind Auszahlungen hoher Beträge (z.B. Steuerzahlungen) sowie Ausgleichszahlungen am Jahresende verantwortlich. Mit dem durchschnittlichen operativen Cashflow von 1,5 Milliarden US-Dollar pro Quartal sind wir *jedoch* höchst zufrieden (PT-SHARE).

   c.   Dieser Cash Flow fällt zwar aufgrund von hohen Barauslagen, wie Steuern und Ausgleichszahlungen am Jahresende, in jedem Quartal unterschiedlich aus, *dennoch* waren wir mit unserem durchschnittlichen jährlichen Cash Flow aus laufenden Geschäftstätigkeiten von 1,5 Millionen $ pro Quartal zufrieden (CAT-SHARE).

   d.   Und basiert *während* dieses von Viertel zu das Viertel schwankt, das auf grossen Barauslagen wie Steuerzahlungen und Jahresendeausgleichszahlungen, wurden wir mit unserem durchschnittlichen positiven Cashflow für das Jahr von den Operationen von $1,5 Milliarde pro Viertel gefallen (RBMT-SHARE).

   e.   Und *während* dies von Quartal zu Quartal basierend auf grosse Barauslagen wie Steuer-Zahlungen und End-of-Jahres-Ausgleichszahlungen variieren, wurden wir mit unserer durchschnittlichen positiven Cashflow für das Jahr aus dem operativen Geschäft von 1,5 Milliarden Dollar pro Quartal (SMT1-SHARE).

   f.   Und *während* diese je nach Viertel bis Viertel auf der Grundlage grosse Geld ausgegeben wie Steuerzahlungen und abschliessende Entschädigung payments, freuen wir uns mit unseren durchschnittliche positive Cashflow für das Jahr von Maßnahmen der $1.5 Milliarden pro quarter (SMT2-SHARE).

In some cases, cohesion might be expressed with different cohesive devices in the two languages under analysis. For instance, the conjunction "while" in the source sentence in example (5) is substituted with a reference expressed with the pronominal adverb *dabei* in PT, see (5-b). Pronominal adverbs expressing a reference are typical for German and are rare in English. At the same time, we observe the adoption of the cohesive device used in the source sentence also in other translation variants (c. to f.).

(5) a. My father preferred to stay in a bathrobe and be waited on for a change *while* he lead the stacks of newspapers me and my grandmother saved for him (EO-FICTION).

    b. Mein Vater ist lieber im Bademantel geblieben und hat sich zur Abwechslung mal bedienen lassen und *dabei* die Zeitungsstapel durchgelesen, die ich und meine Großmutter für ihn aufgehoben haben (PT-FICTION).

    c. Mein Vater saß die ganze Zeit im Bademantel da und ließ sich zur Abwechslung bedienen, *während* er die Zeitungen laß, die meine Großmutter und ich für ihn aufgehoben hatten (CAT-FICTION).

    d. Mein Vater bevorzugt, um in einem Bademantel zu bleiben und auf eine Änderung, *während* er die Stapel von Zeitungen ich und meine führt Großmutter an gewartet zu werden gerettet für ihn (RBMT-FICTION).

    e. Mein Vater lieber im Bademantel bleiben und werden wartete auf eine Veränderung, *während* er die Stapel von Zeitungen mich und meine Großmutter für ihn gerettet führen (SMT1-FICTION).

    f. My Vater lieber Aufenthalt in einem bathrobe und gewartet werden über einen Klimawandel, *während* er die Stapeln kramen Zeitungen für mich und meine Großmutter him (SMT2-FICTION).

In terms of reference, translations demonstrate less noun phrases filled with pronouns than their source texts in English: 137.76 (Trans-$\bar{x}$) vs. 204.14 (EO), whereas the opposite phenomenon is observed, if we compare them to the original texts in German. In this case, we observe more pronominal reference in translations than in comparable originals (137.76 vs. 127.14). However, variation is observed across translation variants: while in human translations pronominal reference is much higher and tends to the values of EO, machine translation shows values which are lower when compared to both EO and GO. This low value is obviously caused by the small amount of pronominal phrases in SMT2. Here, we suppose that many pronouns remained untranslated in certain registers, as seen in example (5-f) above, and were wrongly tagged in the part-of-speech annotation. Moreover, we observe a high number of pronominal references in PT (232.76), which contradicts the hypothesis in §2.3.

The figures obtained for general nouns confirm our hypothesis about their low frequency in translations. On average, translations demonstrate a lower amount of general nouns than EO and GO (20.51 vs. 48.71 and 23.85 respectively). RBMT is the only translation variant whose distribution of general nouns is similar to that of GO. As seen from the values for the originals, there are more general nouns in EO than in GO. This means that this type of nouns is more typical for English than for German. Hence, we observe normalisation in terms of general nouns in all translation variants of our corpus.

In the analysis of explicitation in translations from English into German, one should also take into account the fact that German is more explicit than English, which could also have influenced on the results obtained.

4.2.1 Normalisation and "shining through"

To analyse normalisation and "shining through", we extracted all occurrences of nominal and prepositional phrases and compared them with the occurrences of verbal phrases. Table 4 demonstrates the proportions of nominal (nominal and prepositional phrases) and verbal (verbal phrases) classes across all subcorpora under analysis. As already mentioned in §2.3 above, German is less "verbal" than English, which is confirmed in our data: GO contains less verbal phrases than EO.

The mean value of verbal phrases for all translations comprises 28.63, which is much lower than that of GO. This indicates the phenomenon of normalisation in this case. Comparing the values across translation variants, we observe variation in the degree of normalisation – it is less pronounced in human than in machine translation (33.59 vs. 24.64 respectively). Moreover, human translations produced by professionals are very close to German originals in terms of the distribution of nominal vs. verbal phrases, which means that they demonstrate neither normalisation nor "shining through" if we consider the indicators under analysis.

The higher noun-verb-ratio (NVratio in Table 4) is observed for SMT2. The reason for it could once again be the erroneous part-of-speech tagging which results from the gaps in training data used for SMT2. Most untranslated verbs (e.g. promote, report, import) or verbal forms (recognising, closing, helping, etc.) were tagged as nouns or adjectives.

Overall, the results are rather surprising. Analysing examples in our corpus, we notice that source verbal phrases in human translations from English into German are often translated as nominal phrases, see examples (6-a), (6-b) and

Table 4: Proportionality of nominal vs. verbal opposition in VARTRA-SMALL

subc	nominal	verbal	NVRATIO
EO	59.45	40.55	1.47
GO	61.95	38.05	1.63
PT	61.92	38.08	1.63
CAT	71.87	28.13	2.56
HU-$\bar{x}$	66.41	33.59	1.98
RBMT	72.42	27.58	2.63
SMT1	74.38	25.62	2.90
SMT2	79.54	20.46	3.89
MT-x	75.35	24.64	3.06
Trans-$\bar{x}$	71.36	28.63	2.49

(6-c). However, they are often left as verbal phrases in machine translation, as in examples (6-d), (6-e) and (6-f). Therefore, we would expect machine-produced translations to have a lower noun-verb-ratio, which is not the case in the quantitative data. To analyse the correspondences between source and target phrases we need to align our subcorpora, which is not available at the moment.

(6)   a. Settings *changed* here override settings *changed* anywhere else (EO-INSTR).

      b. Die hier vorgenommenen *Änderungen* setzen alle anderen *Änderungen* außer Kraft (PTINSTR).

      c. Hier vorgenommene Einstellungs*änderungen* sind allen anderen Einstellungs*änderungen* übergeordnet (CAT-INSTR).

      d. Die Einstellungen, die hier *geändert* werden, heben die Einstellungen auf, die irgendwoanders *geändert* werden (RBMT-INSTR).

      e. Hier *geänderten* Einstellungen überschreiben Einstellungen, die anderswo *geändert* (SMT1-INSTR).

      f. … bei dem Sie überhaupt hier über Rahmenbedingungen *geändert* Settings überall else (SMT2-INSTR).

4.3 Convergence

In our last hypothesis, we test if the analysed translations exhibit convergence – the variation of the features across translation variants in our corpus is not high. For this purpose, we consider the indicators analysed in §1, §2 and §3 above: STTR, LD, conj, pronNP, gennoun and Nvratio. The overall variation between the subcorpora is relatively low for all features, except for pronominal reference and noun-verb-ratio (see Figure 1), which means that translation variants in our corpus are alike in terms of the features considered. Most prominent indicators for convergence are that of simplification. We remove pronominal reference and noun-verb-ratio from the data matrix and calculate p–values using the Pearson's chi–square test, which is a univariate statistical method to reveal significant differences between variables. If p–value is < 0.05, then the difference between the compared subcorpora (translation variants) is not significant.

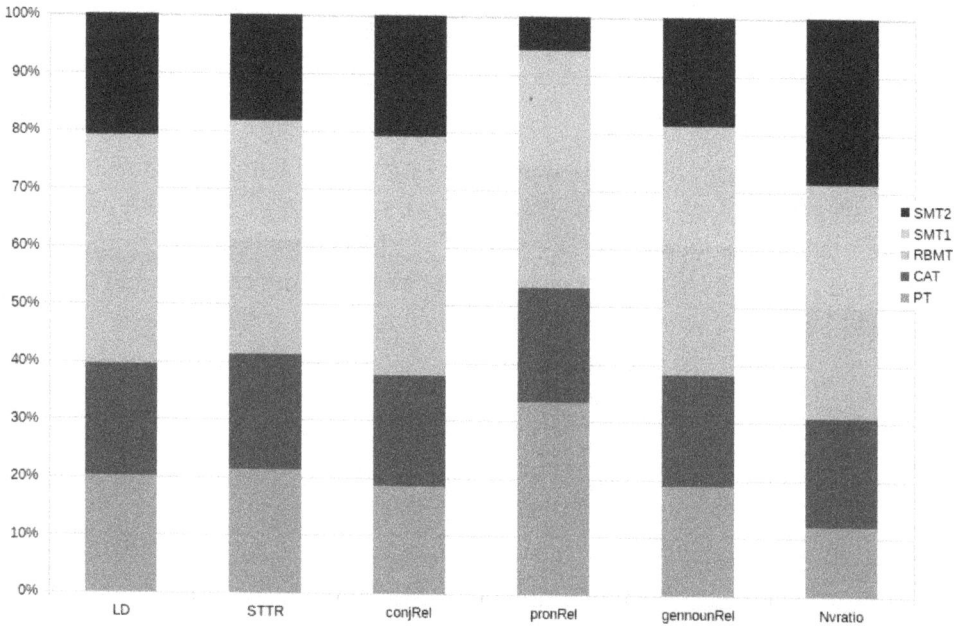

Figure 1: Levelling out in VARTRA-SMALL

We calculate p–value for all pairs of subcorpora in **VARTRA**. The results confirm our assumptions, as p–value is above 0.05 in almost all cases (see Table 5). An exception is pair **PT-SMT2**, where we observe a p–value of approx. 0.01. Our translation variants therefore converge, as expected, as there is no significant difference between almost all subcorpora; they are alike in terms of the analysed

Table 5: p–values for comparison of translation variants

	subc	p–value
PT	VS. CAT	0.8863
	VS. RBMT	0.5663
	VS. SMT1	0.8806
	VS. SMT2	0.0142
CAT	VS. RBMT	0.9307
	VS. SMT1	0.9986
	VS. SMT2	0.0980
RBMT	VS. SMT1	0.9373
	VS. SMT2	0.1771
SMT1	VS. SMT2	0.0731

phenomena, which are indicators of simplification, explicitation and normalisation.

4.4 Summary

Summarising the obtained results, we found that not all hypotheses formulated in §2.3 above can be applied to our dataset. Both type–token–ratio as well as lexical density do not serve as good indicators of simplification in this case. In terms of explicitation, we should also think of further operationalisation, as those chosen reveal rather other phenomena (e.g. normalisation). The hypotheses about normalisation and "shining through" can be confirmed only in part and reflect high variations across translation varieties. The only assumption confirmed by our data is that of convergence. The analysed translation variants converge, as there is no significant difference between them in terms of the analysed phenomena.

5 Conclusion and future work

In this paper, we analysed translation variants produced by humans and machine systems and compared them to their English source texts, as well as comparable German originals. With the help of lexicogrammatical patterns, we were able to trace differences and similarities between them, which indicate the following translation features: simplification, explicitation, normalisation and convergence. Although our analysis includes translations from English into German, we could not detect "shining through" – at least with the indicators at hand. The analysed features vary if we consider translation variants or their groups separately, e.g. in terms of explicitation or normalisation. At the same time, we observe convergence in translation, especially if we take simplification into account.

We believe that we should include more factors into the analysis to explain the variation observed. For example, in some cases, we should revise our hypotheses and their operationalisation, as contrasts between languages should be taken into account. We also need to look at the "experience" factor – this could verify the differences between two human translations observed for some features. Furthermore, restrictions of the translation memory applied in CAT or the training material used in SMT can also have an influence on the distribution of lexico-grammatical patterns. For this, a closer inspection of correlations between translation memory as well as applied SMT training material (parallel corpora) is required, which is planned for our future work.

We also plan to align originals with their translations on word and sentence level to allow analysis of certain phenomena involved, e.g. translation of ambiguous cases, direct translation solutions, see 4.3 and their multiple variants.

Acknowledgments

The project *VARTRA: Translation Variation* was supported by a grant from Forschungsausschuss of the Saarland University.

References

Babych, Bogdan & Tony Hartley. 2004. Extending the BLEU MT Evaluation Method with Frequency Weightings. In *Proceedings of the 42nd annual meeting on association for computational linguistics*, 621–628.

Baker, Mona. 1993. Corpus linguistics and translation studies: Implications and applications. In Mona Baker, Gill Francis & Elena Tognini-Bonelli (eds.), *Text and technology: In honour of John Sinclair*, 233–250. Amsterdam: John Benjamins.

Baker, Mona. 1995. Corpora in translation studies: An overview and some suggestions for future research. *Target* 7(2). 223–243.

Baker, Mona. 1996. Corpus-based translation studies: The challenges that lie ahead. In Harold Somers (ed.), *Terminology, LSP and translation: Studies in language engineering in honour of Juan C. Sager*, 175–186. Amsterdam: John Benjamins.

Baroni, Marco & Silvia Bernardini. 2006. A new approach to the study of translationese: Machine-learning the difference between original and translated text. *Literary and Linguistic Computing* 21(3). 259–274.

Chesterman, Andrew. 2004. Beyond the particular. In Anna Mauranen & Pekka Kujamäki (eds.), *Translation universals: Do they exist?*, 33–49. Amsterdam: John Benjamins.

Dipper, Stefanie, Melanie Seiss & Heike Zinsmeister. 2012. The use of parallel and comparable data for analysis of abstract anaphora in German and English. In Nicoletta Calzolari, Khalid Choukri, Thierry Declerck, Mehmet Ugur Dogan, Bente Maegaard, Joseph Mariani, Jan Odijk & Stelios Piperidis (eds.), *Proceedings of the eight international conference on language resources and evaluation (lrec 2012)*, 138–145. Paris: ELRA.

Evert, Stefan. 2005. *The CQP Query Language Tutorial.* CWB version 2.2.b90. http://www.ims.uni-stuttgart.de/forschung/projekte/CorpusWorkbench/CQPTutorial/cqp-tutorial.2up.pdf.

Frawley, William. 1984. Prolegomenon to a theory of translation. In William Frawley (ed.), *Translation: Literary, Linguistic and Philosophical Perspectives*, 159–175. London: Associated University Press.

Gellerstam, Martin. 1986. Translationese in Swedish novels translated from English. In Lars Wollin & Hans Lindquist (eds.), *Translation Studies in Scandinavia*, 88–95. Lund: CWK Gleerup.

Hansen, Silvia. 2003. *The nature of translated text: An interdisciplinary methodology for the investigation of the specific properties of translations* (Saarbrücken dissertations in computational linguistics and language technology). German Research Center for Artificial Intelligence, Saarland University.

Hansen-Schirra, Silvia, Stella Neumann & Erich Steiner. 2013. *Cross-linguistic corpora for the study of translations. Insights from the language pair English-German*. Berlin: de Gruyter.

Hawkins, John A. 1986. *A comparative typology of English and German*. London: Croom Helm.

House, Juliane. 1997. *Translation quality assessment. A model revisited*. Tübingen: Narr.

Koehn, Philipp, Hieu Hoang, Alexandra Birch, Chris Callison-Burch, Marcello Federico, Nicola Bertoldi, Brooke Cowan, Wade Shen, Christine Moran, Richard Zens, Chris Dyer, Ondrej Bojar, Alexandra Constantin & Evan Herbst. 2007.

Moses: Open source toolkit for statistical machine translation. In *Proceedings of acl-2007*, 177–180. Prague.

Koppel, Moshe & Noam Ordan. 2011. Translationese and its dialects. *Proceedings of the 49th Annual Meeting of the Association for Computational Linguistics (ACL'11)*.

Kunz, Kerstin & Ekaterina Lapshinova-Koltunski. 2014. Cohesive conjunctions in English and German: Systemic contrasts and textual differences. In Caroline Gentens, Ditte Kimps & Lieven Vandelanotte (eds.), *Advances in corpus compilation and corpus applications*. Rodopi.

Kurokawa, David, Cyril Goutte & Pierre Isabelle. 2009. Automatic detection of translated text and its impact on machine translation. In *Proceedings of mt-summit xii*.

König, Ekkehard & Volker Gast. 2007. *Understanding English-German contrasts* (Grundlagen der Anglistik und Amerikanistik). 3rd, extended edition. Berlin: Erich Schmidt Verlag.

Lapshinova-Koltunski, Ekaterina. 2013. VARTRA: A comparable corpus for analysis of translation variation. In *Proceedings of the sixth workshop on building and using comparable corpora*, 77–86. Sofia: Association for Computational Linguistics.

Laviosa, Sara. 1996. *The english comparable corpus (ECC): A resource and a methodology for the empirical study of translation*. Manchester, UK: UMIST PhD thesis.

Laviosa, Sara. 1998. Core patterns of lexical use in a comparable corpus of English narrative prose. In Sara Laviosa (ed.), *The corpus-based approach: A new paradigm in translation studies*, vol. 4 (META XLIII), 474–480.

Laviosa, Sara. 2002. *Corpus-based translation studies: Theory, findings, applications*. Amsterdam: Rodopi.

Lembersky, Gennadi, Noam Ordan & Shuly Wintner. 2012. Language models for machine translation: Original vs. translated texts. *Computational Linguistics* 38(4). 799–825.

Matthiessen, Christian. 2001. The environments of translation. In Erich Steiner & Colin Yallop (eds.), *Exploring translation and multilingual text production: Beyond content*, 41–124. Berlin: de Gruyter.

Mauranen, Anna. 2000. Strange strings in translated language: A study on corpora. In Maeve Olohan (ed.), *Research models in translation studies: Intercultural faultlines: textual and cognitive aspects*, 119–141. Manchaster: St. Jerome Publishing.

Neumann, Stella. 2013. *Contrastive register variation. A quantitative approach to the comparison of English and German*. Berlin: de Gruyter.

Papineni, Kishore, Salim Roukos, Todd Ward & Wei-Jing Zhu. 2002. Bleu: A method for automatic evaluation of machine translation. In *Proceedings of the 40th annual meeting of the association for computational linguistics (acl)*, 311–318.

Popovic, Maja. 2011. Hjerson: An open source tool for automatic error classification of machine translation output. *Prague Bull. Math. Linguistics* 96. 59–68.

Schmid, Helmut. 1994. Probabilistic part-of-speech tagging using decision trees. In *Proceedings of international conference on new methods in language processing*. Manchester, UK.

Steiner, Erich. 2004. *Translated texts: Properties, variants, evaluations*. Frankfurt am Main: Peter Lang.

Steiner, Erich. 2012. A characterization of the resource based on shallow statistics. In Stella Neumann Silvia Hansen-Schirra & Erich Steiner (eds.), *Cross-linguistic corpora for the study of translations: Insights from the language pair English-German*. Berlin: de Gruyter.

Teich, Elke. 2003. *Cross-linguistic variation in system and text: A methodology for the investigation of translations and comparable texts*. Berlin: de Gruyter.

Toury, Gideon. 1995. *Descriptive translation studies and beyond*. Amsterdam: John Benjamins.

White, John S. 1994. The ARPA MT evaluation methodologies: Evolution, lessons, and further approaches. In *Proceedings of the 1994 Conference of the Association for Machine Translation in the Americas*, 193–205.

Chapter 6

Non-human agents in subject position: Translation from English into Dutch: A corpus-based translation study of "give" and "show"

Steven Doms

In English, sentences with action verbs like *give* or *show* can have non-human subjects that play the agent role. Non-human instances of agents are, however, less frequently attested in Dutch (see e.g. Delsoir 2011; Vandepitte & Hartsuiker 2011). Dutch seems to impose restrictions on non-human instances, which do not contain all five proto-agent properties proposed by Dowty (1991). Hence, I expect that translators will not (always) translate English non-human agents as subjects of *give* and *show* with Dutch non-human agents as subjects of the Dutch cognates of *give* and *show*, *geven* and *tonen*, respectively. The choices translators make are described both on a syntactic and semantic level. The translation data of source-text sentences with *give* and source-text sentences with *show* are compared as to verify whether these source-text verbs give rise to different solutions proposed by translators.

1 Introduction

English sentences such as (1a) and (2a) contain multiple participants, of which only one participant, to wit the agent, fulfills the grammatical function of subject and performs the action denoted by the verb *give* and *show*, respectively. In (1a), two other participants can be discerned apart from the non-human agent (*an agreement which*): a recipient who receives something from the agent (*Interbrew*) and a theme which is given to the recipient by the agent (*a 24% stake in China's*

Steven Doms. 2014. Non-human agents in subject position: Translation from English into Dutch: a corpus-based translation study of "give" and "show". In Claudio Fantinuoli & Federico Zanettin (eds.), *New directions in corpus-based translation studies*, 99–119. Berlin: Language Science Press *fifth largest and most profitable brewer*). In total, this example counts three participants, making it a trivalent sentence. Example (2a), on the other hand, exemplifies a divalent sentence with a non-human agent (*Studies in animals*) and a theme (*reproductive toxicity*). All examples given in this paper are taken from the Dutch Parallel Corpus (DPC) (see Rura, Vandeweghe & Perez 2008), except indicated otherwise. Subjects are marked in bold and verbs are underlined.

(1)   a. (...) an ⌐agreement⌐ which gives ⌐Interbrew⌐ a 24% stake in ⌐China⌐'s fifth largest and most profitable brewer.

      b. Met de ⌐ondertekening⌐ van deze overeenkomst ... verwerft ⌐Interbrew⌐ een particpatie van 24% in ⌐China⌐'s vijfde grootste brouwer
with the signature of this agreement (...) Interbrew acquires a particpation of 24% in China's fifth largest brewer

(2)   a. ⌐Studies in animals⌐ have shown ⌐reproductive toxicity⌐

      b. Uit ⌐experimenteel onderzoek bij dieren⌐ is ⌐reproductietoxiciteit⌐ gebleken
from experimental research on animals **reproductive toxicity** has become apparent

The English sentences display a non-human agent in subject position. Their Dutch translations in (1b) and (2b), however, do not. In (1b), the subject (*Interbrew*) plays the role of recipient and refers to the source-text recipient. Further, the source-text non-human agent becomes an instrument (*met de ondertekening van deze overeenkomst*), while the source-text theme remains a theme in the Dutch translation. This perspective-change in (1b) is achieved by the introduction of the reception verb *verwerven* (*acquire*) in Dutch. A different perspective-change is attested in (2b), in which the source-text non-human agent (*studies in animals*) is represented as the prepositional object *uit experimenteel onderzoek bij dieren* (*from experimental research on animals*), indicating the origin of a state-of-affairs denoted in this target-text sentence. The source-text theme (*reproductive toxicity*) becomes the target-text subject (*reproductietoxiciteit*), which fulfills the theme role, typical of subjects of state verbs like *blijken uit* (*become apparent from*).

    In this paper, I will investigate how 388 English sentences with non-human agents as subjects of *give* or *show* are translated into Dutch. From a linguistic point of view, I will enquire which solutions are chosen by translators to avoid

Dutch non-human agents. From a translation perspective, Dutch translations of source-text sentences with *give* and source-text sentences with *show* are analyzed separately to verify whether the source-text verb impacts the translation choices opted for by translators. First, however, the concept of non-human agent is described and enclosed in the agent prototype in Section 2.

2 Agents

Agents are participants which perform the action described by particular verbs. In the literature, agents have often been characterized in terms of so-called agentive features which according to Hundt (2004: 49) "entail animacy (or even humanness)", an example of which can be found in Dowty's 1991 theory of prototypical agents (see §2.1). Non-human instances of the agent role, however, do usually not represent these agentive features, which marks them as less prototypical agents. In §2.2, I will zoom in on these non-human agents and their properties.

2.1 Prototypical Agents

In his *Thematic Proto-Roles and Argument Selection*, Dowty (1991: 572) proposes five features for prototypical agents:

- "volitional involvement in the event or state"

- "sentience (and/or perception)"

- "causing an event or change of state in another participant"

- "movement (relative to the position of another participant)"

- "exist independently of the event named by the verb"

These features can be summarized as volition, sentience, causation, movement and independent existence. Agents which have all five proto-agent properties listed by Dowty (1991) are considered prototypical agents like *John* in (3a), in which I assume that *John* acts volitionally and sentiently. This trivalent sentence also includes a recipient (*her*) and a theme (*the book*), so that causation and movement are attested, both of which are related to participants other than the agent. Finally, the agent exists independently of the event in (3a), making it fulfill all five proto-agent properties.

In (3b), however, *Kim* is not an instantiation of a prototypical agent. Although the properties volition, sentience and independent existence are found, causation and movement are not, because the divalent example in (3b) does not contain a recipient. The non-human agent (*the book*) which is the subject of (3c) implies only the proto-agent feature independent existence. Causation and movement fail, because no recipient is attested, while volition and sentience, indeed, seem to be linked to human instances of the agent role.

(3)   a. **John** *gave* her the book yesterday.

       b. **Kim** *gave* blood for the first time yesterday.

       c. **The book** *gave* an overview of historic events in the 21st century.

The examples in (3) illustrate that both human and non-human agents can be instances of less prototypical agents. Non-human agents, however, are per definition less prototypical, because they do not display agentive features such as volition and sentience, which are typical of (some) human agents. In the next section, central attention is given to non-human instances of the agent role.

2.2 Non-Human Agents

In the literature, non-human subjects of action verbs have not always been treated as agents. Several authors (see e.g. Fillmore 1968; Quirk et al. 1972; Levin 1993) consider some of these subjects as instances of the instrument role. *The door* in (4a-b) exemplifies such an instrument that can become subject in sentence (4b), in which there is no agent.

(4)   a. **Dennis** *opened* the door with the key.

       b. **The key** *opened* the door.

Other linguists (see e.g. Biber et al. 1999; Talmy 2000) discern what they call causers, i.e. abstract entities and (natural) forces such as a *biting wind gusting to 30 knots* in Biber et al.'s (1999) example in (5).

(5)   a. **A biting wind gusting to 30 knots** *threatened to blow* the fragile, 15-ft fiberglass hydroplane off course.

In this paper, non-human subjects of action verbs are seen as agents. The agent role is defined as the participant which is the subject of an action verb and which

– following Dowty (1991) – exists independently of the event named by that action verb. This definition of agent allows for a concept of agents/agency which does not a priori presuppose animacy or humanness of the agent role. Hence, the agent role can be further subdivided into human and non-human instances. The source-text non-human agents which are under investigation are subjects of the English action verbs *give* and *show*. How these source-text non-human agents are translated in Dutch is shown in §6. First, however, an account is made of restrictions on non-human agents which seem to exist in Dutch according to earlier research.

3 Constraints on Dutch non-human agents

In some languages, restrictions have been shown to exist on non-human agents as subjects of typical action verbs. This has, for instance, been demonstrated for German (see e.g. Bahns 1993), Spanish (see e.g. Slabakova & Montrul 2002) and some Asian languages (see e.g. Master 1991). Recently, studies have been conducted to determine whether such constraints also exist in Dutch. In this section, the focus lies on four recent studies in which Dutch translations of English non-human agents have been investigated.

The first study to be discussed here originates from Vandepitte (2007), who focuses on the translation techniques one particular translator used in translating 300 English sentences containing a non-human agent into Dutch. These source-text and target-text sentences were part of an approximately 70,000 word parallel corpus which was compiled from Hertz's ESSAY *The Silent Takeover* and its Dutch translation *De Stille Overname*. Vandepitte distinguishes between four translation techniques: *no semantic or pragmatic differences between source and target text, implicitation* (i.e. those cases in which the target-text sentence is more implicit than the source-text sentence), *explicitation* (i.e. those cases in which the target-text sentence is more explicit than the source-text sentence) *and other semantic or pragmatic changes*, which is in most instances a combination of both implicitation and explicitation.

Vandepitte reports that in about one third of the Dutch translations, no semantic or pragmatic differences are attested between source-text and target-text sentences. Two thirds of the translations, on the other hand, display shifts. Explicitation occurs in less than one out of ten target-text sentences, whereas one out of four target-text sentences can be seen as an instance of implicitation. About one third of the 300 instances examined by Vandepitte (2007) show other semantic or pragmatic changes. These results reveal that translation of non-human agents into Dutch leads to (especially) semantic and (sometimes) pragmatic changes. This study, however, does not zoom in on the semantics of the non-human agents themselves, as opposed to D'haeyere's (2010) inquiry.

D'haeyere identifies "non-prototypical agents with prototypical agent requiring predicates", which are abbreviated as NPAPARPs, a term coined by Vandepitte (2010). These abstract and non-human agents as subjects of verbs that typically take a human agent are searched in a set of 200 English sentences. The way in which these English source-text sentences are translated in Dutch is investigated in order to establish whether Dutch non-human agents are avoided. D'haeyere (2010) discerns three possible ways in which translators can deal with NPAPARPs: similar translation of the NPAPARP, different translation of the NPAPARP or no NPAPARP in Dutch.

Her findings suggest that in little more than half of all translations, translators opted to maintain the NPAPARPs in Dutch, in which cases the NPAPARPs were most often translated similarly and only sometimes different vis-à-vis the source text. In the other half of the instances, however, the Dutch translations no longer contained NPAPARPs. D'haeyere describes shifts which were used to avoid NPAPARPs in Dutch. In almost half of these instances, NPAPARPs are transformed into Dutch prepositional phrases, i.e. into translations which do no longer contain a verb, but a preposition which links the other lexical elements. Further, in about one out of ten Dutch translations NPAPARPs have disappeared, because copular verbs are used. Two other frequent shifts are the introduction of human agents and agent ellipsis. Finally, in some instances, the use of a state or content verb or a conditional clause are attested.

D'haeyere's results indicate that it is the verb that is adapted most often to avoid Dutch non-human agents. In those cases in which Dutch translations contain a non-human agent, mainly causative verbs like *zorgen voor* (*cause*) are found. Furthermore, D'haeyere's data show that Dutch non-human agents more often refer to concrete objects, whereas more abstract entities are found in the source-text sentences.

As opposed to Vandepitte (2007) and D'haeyere (2010), Vandepitte & Hartsuiker (2011) do not focus on the product of translation, but on the translation process. In an experimental study, they inquire into the extent to which NPAPARPs result in higher translation processing costs than prototypical (human) agents. To verify this, a test is built which consists of seventy-six English sentences – thirty-eight with a prototypical agent and thirty-eight with a non-prototypical agent – which have to be translated in Dutch by trained (master students) and untrained (first-year bachelor students) translators. In total, twenty-four translators

– fourteen trained and ten untrained – provide comparable results. The experiment shows that untrained translators translate English non-human agents with Dutch non-human agents in approximately 83% of the instances, while trained translators maintain non-prototypical agents in about 73% of the Dutch translations.

Besides this "very strong tendency to translate constructions with a non-prototypical agent with a construction that similarly has a non-prototypical agent", Vandepitte & Hartsuiker (2011: 11) also find that English sentences with non-prototypical agents are translated slower by both trained and untrained translators, which makes them conclude that NPAPARPs constitute a translation process problem.

Finally, Delsoir (2011) used Vandepitte & Hartsuiker's 2011 data to investigate which NPAPARPs are accepted in Dutch and which are not. Delsoir has 226 respondents rate twenty-eight Dutch translations of English NPAPARPs in terms of acceptability. In total, nine translations are rated unacceptable, fourteen translations are found to be sufficiently acceptable and only five translations receive the label acceptable in Dutch. Delsoir argues that the Dutch verbs in the translations at least "partly have volition as a feature, and therefore should require a prototypical agent" Vandepitte & Hartsuiker (2011: 34), leading him to the conclusion that English has been leaking into Dutch on a grammatical level.

The findings in these four studies are based on English source-text sentences and their Dutch translations which contain verbs belonging to different semantic verb types which typically call for very specific syntactic patterns. In the present study, however, the English source-text sentences only include two verbs: *give* and *show*, for each of which a detailed semantic and syntactic description is given in §4.

4 *Give* and *show*

In this study, all source-text non-human agents are subjects of either *give* or *show*. *Give* as well as *show* typically calls for a human agent subject which conducts a (non-)material transfer of a theme to(wards) a recipient. These two trivalent verbs which are frequently attested in the Dutch Parallel Corpus (see also §5), however, also allow for non-human agents in subject position, as was illustrated by the examples in (1) and (2), so that they are expected to yield sufficient English source-text sentences with non-human agents in subject position, of which the Dutch translations will be analyzed and compared. Both English verbs are treated in detail below.

4.1 *Give*

Give is a trivalent verb which expresses an act in which an agent hands over a theme to a recipient. The agent initiates the action and typically becomes subject, while the theme has the grammatical function of direct object and the recipient is the indirect object, as was illustrated by example (1a) in the introduction. Although *give* can call for three participants (agent, theme, recipient), it can also occur in sentences which portray only two participants (agent and theme, but no recipient), as in (3b-c). In §2.1, it has been demonstrated that the absence of the recipient has an impact on the prototypicality of the agent. Since in this paper I zoom in on one particular type of agent, i.e. the non-human agent, which can be considered an agent which includes only one of the five proto-agent properties listed by Dowty (1991), I will not limit myself to instances with three participants. Both divalent and trivalent English source-text sentences with non-human agents as subjects of *give* are taken into account.

4.2 *Show*

The English verb *show* resembles *give* in that it allows for three participants: an agent, a theme and a recipient. In a trivalent sentence with *show*, the agent shows the recipient a theme, as in the nominal relative clause in (6a), in which the non-human agent (*one simple concept that*) fulfills the grammatical function of subject, the recipient (*us*) is the indirect object and the theme (*the way forward*) functions as grammatical direct object. The theme may occur as a noun phrase like in (6a), but can, for instance, also take the form of a *that*-clause like in (6b). As it was the case for *give*, *show* can also be found in divalent sentences such as (2a), in which there is no recipient. Dutch translations of both divalent and trivalent sentences with *show* are investigated.

(6) a. There is **one simple concept that** <u>shows</u> us the way forward
     b. **The salon** <u>showed</u> people that we did wash our hair

Before analyzing the Dutch translations of English source-text sentences containing *give* and *show*, the method of selecting the data underlying this study is presented in §5.

5 Corpus: data and methodology

In order to procure English source-text sentences with non-human agents as subjects of *give* and *show*, the lemmas "give" and "show" were searched in the 10 million word sentence-aligned Dutch Parallel Corpus (DPC) of English, French and Dutch (see e.g. Rura, Vandeweghe & Perez 2008),[1] which comprises five text types: literature, instructive, journalistic, administrative texts and external communication. This search yielded 1986 English sentences with *give* (1208) and *show* (778) lemmas. Further filtering of these sentences was required. First, all English source-text sentences which did not have a Dutch translation – for reasons unknown to me – were left out as well as source-text sentences which occurred more than once with identical translations, in which case only one English-Dutch translation pair was maintained. Furthermore, source-text sentences were attested in which *give* and *show* did not denote the verb meanings described in §4. Hence, instances containing phrasal verbs (e.g. *give in, show up*), expressions (e.g. *give someone the eye, show one's hand*) and idioms (e.g. *give birth to, show face*) were also filtered out. These first two filterings eventually leave us with 1220 instances.

Not all of these 1220 instances, however, have an agent as their subject. Passive sentences and source-text sentences without subjects (e.g. past participial, prepositional, infinitival clauses as well as nominalizations and adjectives) received the label "no agent", as shown in Table 1. The other instances have a subject which represents the agent role. A difference was then made between source-text sentences with a human and a non-human agent. Table 1 shows how often source-text sentences with *give* and *show* contained no, a human or a non-human agent.

Table 1: Instances with and without agents

	Give	%	*Show*	%	Total	%
No Agent	376	48.3	98	22.2	474	38.9
Human Agent	248	31.9	110	24.9	358	29.3
Non-Human Agent	154	19.8	234	52.9	388	31.8
Total	778	63.8	442	36.2	1220	100

The results in Table 1 reveal that about half of the source-text sentences with *give* do not include agents, while this is true for only about a fifth of the source-text sentences with *show*. If the attestations of *give* and *show* in agentless instances are left out of consideration, both verb queries in the DPC seem to yield

---

[1] A search interface for the DPC was created by I. Delaere and A. Malfait, to whom I am greatly indebted

a comparable number of source-text sentences which are headed by agent sub-jects. *Give*, however, preferably takes human agents as its subjects, whereas *show* is attested especially with non-human agent subjects. In total, 388 instances, i.e. approximately a third of all attested source-text sentences, contain a non-human agent as subject of *give* or *show*. In §6, a detailed analysis is made of the ways in which these source-text sentences have been translated into Dutch.

6 Data analysis

In these sections, I will elaborate on the Dutch translations of 154 source-text sentences with non-human agents as subjects of *give* and 234 source-text sen-tences with non-human agents as subjects of *show*. In §6.1, the way in which the source-text non-human agents are translated in Dutch is investigated. The choices translators make to avoid Dutch non-human agents are described in §6.2.

6.1 Dutch translations of non-human agents

As reported in §3, Dutch has been shown to have restrictions on non-human agents in subject position. In this section, Dutch translations of English source-text non-human agents are examined to determine how often English non-human agents as subjects of *give* and *show* are translated with Dutch non-human agents. Table 2 shows what happens with the 388 source-text non-human agents in Dutch translations.

Table 2: Dutch translations of English non-human agents

	EN non-human agent: give	%	EN non-human agent: show	%	Total	%
NL non-human agent	92	59.7	130	55.5	222	57.2
NL human agent	10	6.5	17	7.3	27	7
NL no agent	52	33.8	87	37.2	139	35.8
Total	154	39.7	234	60.3	388	100

As Table 2 demonstrates, in about 57% of the Dutch translations, non-human agents are attested in subject position. This number of Dutch non-human agents corresponds more or less to D'haeyere (2010) findings, which showed non-human agents in slightly more than half of 200 Dutch translations. Almost 60% of the source-text sentences with *give* result in Dutch translations with non-human agents, while almost 55% of the source-text sentences with *show* give birth to Dutch translations with non-human agents.

In all these instances, the source-text non-human agents have been translated literally or similarly into Dutch and the source-text verbs *give* and *show* have been translated with their Dutch cognates *geven* or *tonen,* as in (7b) and (8b), or with other Dutch action verbs like *bieden* (*offer*) in (9b) or the Dutch verbal collocation *in kaart brengen* (*map out*) in (10b) which typically call for an agent as their subject.

(7) a. The (annual report) gives a true and fair view of the (results) of the
company

   b. Het (jaarverslag) geeft een getrouw overzicht van de (resultaten)
van het bedrijf
the annual report gives a true overview of the results of the company

(8) a. An (X-ray) showed two (foreign bodies)

   b. Een (röntgenfoto) toonde twee (vreemde objecten)
an x-ray showed two foreign objects

(9) a. The (World Expo) gives (us) the (chance) to meet customers

   b. **De** (Wereldexpo) zal (ons) de (mogelijkheid) bieden bestaande
klanten te ontmoeten
the World Expo will offer us the possibility to meet existing
customers

(10)   a.   **Our** (study) shows for the first time the (entire process)

   b.   **Onze** (studie) brengt voor de allereerste keer het (hele proces) in
   kaart
   our study maps out for the very first time the entire process

Although translators have opted for verbs which typically take agents as their subjects, only 7% of the Dutch translations have a subject that plays the agent role and at the same time refers to a human referent. If translators did decide to avoid Dutch (non-human) agents, other solutions were chosen. These solutions which lead to Dutch translations without non-human agents are illustrated and given center stage in the next section.

6.2 Dutch translations without non-human agents

More than forty percent of all Dutch translations include a subject that is not a non-human agent. Translators have produced very diverse translations which can be grouped here as three main solutions to avoid Dutch non-human agents: introduction of a human agent, use of a non-agentive subject or omission of the verb. Table 3 shows how often translators used each of these solutions.

Table 3: Solutions used to avoid NL non-human agents

	EN non-human agent: *give*		EN non-human agent: *show*		Total	%
	abs	%	abs	%		
NL non-human agent subject	10	16.1	17	16.4	27	16.3
NL non-agentive subject	47	75.8	75	72.1	122	73.5
NL no verb	5	8.1	12	11.5	17	10.2
Total	62	37.3	104	62.7	166	100

As Table 3 indicates, translators' choice to avoid Dutch non-human agents mainly results in target-text sentences with a non-agentive subject. Both the introduction of a Dutch human agent (in about 16% of these translations) and omission of verb in Dutch (in about 10% of these translations) explain what happens in the remaining quarter of the Dutch translations without non-human agents in subject position. All three solutions have different ways of realization which are dealt with in the following sections. In §6.2.1, instances with Dutch human agents are discussed in detail, while §6.2.2 zooms in on instances with Dutch non-agentive subjects. In §6.2.3, Dutch translations without a verb are dealt with.

6.2.1 Introduction of a human agent

A first solution adopted by translators in less than one in ten translations (see Table 2 and Table 3, §6.1 and §6.2) consists of introducing a Dutch human agent. This solution can be realized in two different ways. Either translators translate source-text sentences literally (or similarly), except for the source-text non-human agent which is replaced with a human(ized) agent in Dutch, like *institutional* "*power-grabbing*" in (11a) which is translated with the collective noun *instellingen* (*institutions*) in (11b) or like the *pictures* which become *hij* (*he*), thus unveiling the metonymic relation between a product in (12a) and its producer in (12b).

(11)   a.   **Institutional** ("power-grabbing") will give the (Convention) a (bad name)

      b.   **Instellingen die** ("machtsbelust") **optreden** geven de (Conventie) een (slechte naam)
          institutions that act power-hungry give the Convention a bad name

(12)   a.   (The pictures) show the (aftermath of the battle)

      b.   (Hij) toont het (naspel van de veldslag)
          he shows the aftermath of the battle

In other instances, however, translators have not only introduced a human agent in the Dutch translations, but also replaced the source-text verb *give* or *show* with another action verb. In (13), the source-text non-human agent *this agreement* is translated as a prepositional object in Dutch, while the source-text recipient *us* becomes the subject in the target text. This human subject plays the agent role of the Dutch verb *verkopen* (*sell*), which is preceded by the modal verb *kunnen* (*can*). In this instance, the source-text sentence is trivalent, whereas the target-text sentence only counts two participants.

In (14), the target-text sentence also reveals a human agent: *een presentatrice met een grote hoofddoek* (*a female presenter with a big headscarf*). The source-text subject, however, referred to the non-human agent *the television* which occurs as an adverbial in the Dutch translation. The source-text verb *show* has been replaced with Dutch *lezen* (*read*) which calls for a theme as its direct object, in this case *het nieuws* (*the news*) which was part of the source-text direct object, but solely becomes the target-text direct object. In this example, both source-text and target-text sentence exhibit a divalent structure. Although the divalent structure in both sentences is very different, all source-text elements are represented in the Dutch translation. This tendency can also be distilled from the two other solutions translators have opted for to avoid Dutch non-human agents in subject position.

(13) a. This ⟨agreement⟩ gives ⟨us⟩ highly-valued ⟨brands⟩

     b. Door deze ⟨overeenkomst⟩ kunnen ⟨we⟩ ⟨merken⟩ verkopen
        through this agreement **we** can sell brands

(14) a. (...) **the** ⟨television⟩ showing a ⟨female ⟨news⟩ presenter⟩ in full hijab

     b. Op de ⟨televisie⟩ leest een ⟨presentratrice⟩ met een grote **hoofddoek** het ⟨nieuws⟩

        on the television **a female presenter with a big headscarf** reads the news

6.2.2 Use of a non-agentive subject

In more than a third of all Dutch translations (see Table 2), translators choose a Dutch subject which does not play the agent role. Instead, these Dutch subjects denote the semantic role of another participant such as theme, possessor or recipient. Table 4 shows how often each of these non-agentive roles occurred as subjects of Dutch translations.

    The non-agentive role that occurs most often as subject in these Dutch translations is theme. Especially in translations of source-text sentences with *show*, theme subjects are very frequently attested. The introduction of Dutch theme subjects is achieved through two ways: either by using a Dutch state verb like *zijn* (*be*), as in (15b), or by using the passive voice, as in (16b), which gives rise to theme subjects as well.

Table 4: Dutch translations with non-agentive subjects

	Source-text sentences					
	with *give*	%	with *show*	%	Total	%
NL theme subject	25	53.2	70	93.3	95	77.9
NL possessor subject	7	14.9	5	6.7	12	9.8
NL recipient subject	15	31.9	0	0	15	12.3
Total	47	38.5	75	61.5	122	100

(15) a. **The** (doctrine) gave a (younger generation) a
(way of thinking)

 b. (Rasta) was voor de (jongere generaties) een
(nieuwe manier van denken)

 Rasta was for the younger generation a new way of thinking

(16) a. (Animal studies) have shown that (exposure) decreases

 b. In (dieronderzoeken) is aangetoond dat (blootstelling) afneemt
in animal studies it has been shown **that exposure decreases**

The target-text subject *rasta* in (15b) refers to the source-text subject *the doctrine*, but translator's choice for the target-text verb *zijn* entails that *rasta* plays the theme role. Further, *zijn* not only calls for different semantic participants than *give*, but also has a different syntactic pattern. While (15a) is a trivalent sentence, (15b) cannot have three participants framed in one subject and two object positions. Therefore, the source-text recipient *a younger generation* becomes a beneficiary in the Dutch translation, preceded by the preposition *voor* (*for*).

In (16), on the other hand, the target-text subject is a theme subject, due to passivization. The use of the passive voice gives birth to a different syntactic and semantic pattern in the Dutch translation (16b) vis-à-vis English sentence (16a). The source-text subject *animal studies* is part of an adverbial in Dutch, whereas the source-text theme *that exposure decreases* is the target-text theme subject. (16a) is a divalent sentence, (16b) is monovalent, with a prepositional phrase indicating the origin of the assumption made in the target-text theme subject. In both (15) and (16), however, all lexical information of the source-text sentences is represented in the target-text sentences.

Apart from theme subjects, Dutch translations also contain subjects that play the semantic role of possessor. These possessor subjects occur if *give* or *show* are translated with a Dutch possession verb like *bezitten* (*possess*) in (17b) or *hebben* (*have*) in (18b).

(17)   a.   **InBev has** (complementary) skills, giving the (company) (world-class capabilities)

   b.   (...) (waardoor) **de** (onderneming) (eersteklas capaciteiten) bezit
        whereby the company possesses first-class capabilities

(18)   a.   What (benefit) has (ProMeris) shown during the studies?

   b.   Welke (voordeelen) bleek (ProMeris) tijdens de studies te hebben?
        what benefits **ProMeris** turned out to have during the studies?

Target-text sentence (17b) not only differs from source-text sentence (17a) in the way in which *give* is translated. The source-text subject which takes the form of a clause (*InBev has complementary skills*) is found as the pronominal adverb *waardoor* (*whereby*) in Dutch, while the source-text recipient *the company* becomes subject in the target text. In (18), the source-text subject (*ProMeris*) also functions as subject in Dutch, albeit as a possessor instead of a non-human agent. Further, the Dutch verb *hebben* (*have*) is preceded by the verb *blijken* (*turn out*) which adds a degree of modality to target-text sentence (18b).

Finally, in almost one in ten Dutch translations of source-text sentences with *give*, recipient subjects are attested. These subjects do not occur in translations of source-text sentences with *show*. This might not be surprising, since verbs like *krijgen* (*get*) in (19b) actually depict the act of giving from a different angle, i.e. from the opposite perspective in which a recipient receives a theme from an agent.

(19) a. **People [are]** (smoking) **behind me and that** <u>gives</u> (me) an
      (asthma attack)

   b. Mensen achter mij zitten te (roken), waardoor (ik) een
      (astma-aanval) krijg
      people behind me are smoking, whereby I <u>get</u> an asthma attack

The perspective-change which takes place in (19) gives birth to the Dutch recipient subject *ik* (*me*) which can be brought back to the source-text recipient. The
source-text subject, a non-human agent representing a clause, is portrayed in
Dutch by the pronominal adverb *waardoor* (*whereby*) which refers to the source-
text situation *people [are] smoking behind me.*

6.2.3 Omission of the verb

A third solution to avoid Dutch non-human agents is chosen by translators in
almost five percent of all Dutch translations and leads to a target-text sentence
which does not contain a verb, as is illustrated in (20b) and (21b). Various ways
exist through which this solution can be established. In (20b), the source-text
verb *give* is replaced in the target text with the preposition *in*. This type of translation is what D'haeyere (2010) refers to as transformation into a prepositional
phrase. *Show*, on the other hand, is left untranslated in (21b). Instead, colons are
introduced. In both (20b) and (21b) the lack of target-text verb engenders that no
target-text subject is attested either.

(20) a. (...) the (women pickers) **whose generalised**
      (clothing) gave **them a** (timeless) **quality**

   b. (...) (olijvenpluksters) in eenvoudige, (tijdloze)
      (kleding) women olive pickers in simple, timeless clothing

(21) a. **2002** (results) <u>shows</u> **11.5%** (organic operating profit growth)

   b. (Resultaten) 2002: interne groei (bedrijfsresultaat) van 11.5%
      results 2002: organic operating profit growth of 11.5%

7 Discussion

The Dutch translations produced by translators who translated 388 English sentences with non-human agents as subjects of *give* and *show* seem to indicate that most lexical information stored in the source-text sentences is also displayed in the target-text sentences. Almost sixty percent of the target-text sentences contain non-human agents in subject position. In these instances, the lexical source-text information is mostly represented in word-for-word translations. In the other forty percent, however, the syntactic and semantic patterns of the source-text sentences are not followed. Nevertheless, most of these instances likewise reveal a tendency to represent the lexical information denoted by the source-text sentences throughout the Dutch translations.

In the forty percent Dutch translations which avoid non-human agents, especially semantic changes are attested, rather than explicitations or implicitations (see Vandepitte 2007). These changes in the target-text sentences often lead to differences in valency vis-à-vis the respective source texts. As the findings in Table 5 show, English non-human agent subjects of *give* are attested especially in trivalent (agent, theme, recipient) and only in less than third of the instances in divalent (agent and theme) source-text sentences.

The opposite tendency is found for the source-text sentences with non-human agent subjects of *show*, which are almost exclusively divalent. This difference in the valency patterns of both source-text verbs may to some extent be brought back to their semantic nature: *give* is typically referred to as a dative verb, i.e. a verb which typically takes a recipient indirect object, while *show* is a lexical causative of the typically divalent verb *see*, thus giving it the sense of *make see*, the valency pattern of which not necessarily calls for a recipient direct object.

Table 5: Valency reduction in Dutch translations

	EN trivalent give	%	EN divalent give	%	EN trivalent show	%	EN divalent show	%	Total	%
NL trivalent	53	47.8	0	0	2	40	0	0	55	14.2
NL divalent	44	39.6	32	74.4	3	60	145	63.3	224	57.7
NL monovalent	10	9	10	23.3	0	0	72	31.4	92	23.7
NL avalent	4	3.6	1	2.3	0	0	12	5.2	17	4.4
Total	111	28.6	43	11.1	5	1.3	229	59	388	100

As Table 5 also reveals, trivalent source-text instances of *give* are translated especially with Dutch trivalent (47.8%) and divalent (39.6%) target-text sentences and occasionally with Dutch monovalent (9%) and even avalent (3.6) constructions. English divalent source-text sentences of *give* are translated in approximately three quarters of the instances with Dutch divalent target-text sentences and in almost a quarter of the instances with Dutch monovalent target-text sentences. The divalent source-text sentences of *show* display a similar translation pattern, as they are translated in almost two thirds of the instances with Dutch divalent target-text sentences, in about a third of the instances with Dutch monovalent target-text sentences, and in some instances even with Dutch avalent constructions.

To sum up, Dutch translations of trivalent (29.9%) and divalent (70.1%) source-text sentences of *give* and *show* are mainly divalent (57.7%) and even monovalent (23.7%), thus indicating a valency reduction in the target-text sentences. This valency reduction, however, does not imply a loss of (lexical) information in the Dutch translations. As revealed throughout §6.2 and its subsections, the instances in which non-human agents are avoided in Dutch show various different distributions of the source-text elements. Shifts in grammatical functions and semantic roles occur very often, giving birth to different valency patterns with regard to the source texts. These shifts, however, are usually not explicitations, nor implicitations, but semantic changes, confirming (Vandepitte 2007) findings.

These changes may also take the edge of Delsoir's 2011 claim that English has been leaking into the Dutch language on a grammatical level. Perhaps, the instances in which Dutch non-human agents are maintained are the result of priming (e.g. Vandepitte & Hartsuiker 2011; Delsoir 2011) or interference from the source texts rather than an effect of the Dutch language's drifting towards Anglo-American language norms (e.g. House 2008). Or perhaps, the present findings reflect the every-day reality of translators who are faced with the problem of having to choose between a primed Dutch translation with a non-human agent in subject position and a Dutch translation without a non-human agent but with a different semantic and syntactic pattern.

8 Conclusion

In this study, I have investigated how 388 English source-text sentences with non-human agents as subjects of *give* and *show* have been translated into Dutch. Although restrictions exist on non-human agents in subject position in Dutch, almost six in ten Dutch translations include a non-human agent. These target-text sentences follow the syntactic and semantic structure of their respective source-text sentences, which are mainly trivalent in case of sentences with *give* and divalent in case of sentences with *show*. On the other hand, three solutions have been proposed by translators to avoid Dutch non-human agents.

First, human agents have been introduced in less than one in ten target-text sentences. In almost a third of all Dutch translations, however, the agent is not humanized, but rather replaced with another participant which plays another semantic role such as theme, possessor or recipient. These target-text sentences are characterized by a variety of syntactic and semantic patterns which differ from the source-text patterns. These changes lead to valency reduction, but not, however, to (lexical) information loss. Finally, in some instances, the verb is omitted in the Dutch translations, so that no target-text participants can be discerned.

Whether the present findings are the result of priming/interference or the impact English has on the Dutch language (see e.g. House 2008; Delsoir 2011) is unclear. Further research might articulate an answer to this question. It is clear, however, that translators have decided between either primed translations with non-human agents and translations without non-human agents, but with specific Dutch syntactic and semantic patterns which differ from those in the English source texts. Further research into original Dutch might also reveal whether the Dutch translations without non-human agents as well as their specific syntactic and semantic patterns are the more typical instances of the Dutch language.

References

Bahns, Jens. 1993. Lexical collocations: A contrastive view. *ELT Journal* 47(1). 56–63.

Biber, Douglas, Stig Johansson, Geoffrey Leech, Susan Conrad & Edward Finegan. 1999. *The Longman grammar of spoken and written English*. London: Longman.

Delsoir, Jan. 2011. *The acceptability of non-prototypical agents with prototypical agent requiring predicates in dutch*. Gent: Hogeschool Gent.

Dowty, David. 1991. Thematic proto-roles and argument selection. *Language* 67(3). 547–619.

D'haeyere, Laurence. 2010. *Non-prototypical agents with proto-agent requiring predicates: A corpus study of their translation from English into Dutch*. Gent: Hogeschool Gent.

Fillmore, Charles J. 1968. The case for case. In E. Bach & R.T. Harms (eds.), *Universals in linguistic theory*, 1–25. London: Holt, Rinehart & Winston.

House, Juliane. 2008. Towards a linguistic theory of translation as re-contextualisation and a Third Space phenomenon. *Linguistica Antverpiensia* 7. 149–175.

Hundt, Marianne. 2004. Animacy, agentivity, and the spread of the progressive in modern English. *English Language and Linguistics* 8. 47–69.

Levin, Beth. 1993. *English verb classes and alternations: A preliminary investigation.* Chicago: University of Chicago Press.

Master, Peter. 1991. Inanimate subjects with active verbs in scientific prose. *English for Specific Purposes* 10(1). 15–33.

Quirk, Randolph, Sidney Greenbaum, Geoffrey Leech & Jan Svartvik. 1972. *A grammar of contemporary English.* London: Longman.

Rura, Lidia, Willy Vandeweghe & Maribel M. Perez. 2008. Designing a parallel corpus as a multifunctional translator's aid. In *Proceedings of the XVIII FIT World Congress.* Shanghai.

Slabakova, Roumyana & Silvina Montrul. 2002. On aspectual shifts in L2 spanish. In Barbora Skarabela, Sarah Fish & Anna H.-J. Do (eds.), *Proceedings of the Boston University conference on language and development*, 631–642. Somerville, MA: Cascadilla Press.

Talmy, Leonard. 2000. *Toward a cognitive semantics* (Vol. 1). Cambridge: The MIT Press.

Vandepitte, Sonia. 2007. Semantic and pragmatic meanings in translation. *Belgian Journal of Linguistics* 21. Vandeweghe, Willy and Van De Velde, Marc and Vandepitte, Sonia, 185–200.

Vandepitte, Sonia. 2010. Implication as a solution for untranslatability: A corpus study of the translation of non-prototypical agents with proto-agent requiring predicates. In *Paper presented at the methodological advances in corpus-based translation studies (mats 2010) conference, University College Ghent (Belgium) January 8 and 9, 2010.* Paper. MATS.

Vandepitte, Sonia & Robert J. Hartsuiker. 2011. Metonymic language use as a student translation problem: Towards a controlled psycholinguistic investigation. In Cecilia Alvstad, Adelina Hild & Elisabet Tiselius (eds.), *Methods and strategies of process research: Integrative approaches in translation studies*, 67–92. Amsterdam: John Benjamins.

Chapter 7

Investigating judicial phraseology with COSPE: A contrastive corpus-based study

Gianluca Pontrandolfo

This chapter describes the results of an empirical study of LSP phraseological units in a specific domain (criminal law) and type of legal genre (criminal judgments). The final goal of the research is to provide legal translators with a multifunctional resource having a positive impact on the translation process and product. More specifically, it aims at assisting translators – as well as legal experts – to develop their phraseological competence through exposure to real, authentic (con)texts in which these phraseological units are used. Based on COSPE, a 6-million trilingual, comparable corpus of criminal judgments, this study approaches phraseology from a contrastive (Spanish-Italian-English), quantitative and qualitative perspective. Corpus analysis and term extraction have been carried out by means of concordancers (mainly WordSmith Tools v. 5.0). From a methodological point of view, the study combines corpus-based and corpus-driven approaches, as well as traditional approaches applied to Language for General Purposes (LGP) phraseology, and more recent distributional studies of Language for Specific Purposes (LSP) and legal phraseology. Emphasis is placed on four categories of phraseological units frequently found in judicial discourse: complex prepositions, lexical doublets and triplets, lexical collocations and routine formulae.

1 Introduction

Legal translation is not only a question of terminology – which is indeed one of the major obstacles legal translators have to face in their daily activity – but also a question of phraseological conventions. Beyond lexical and terminological equivalence, translators have to tackle the additional difficulty of acquiring

Gianluca Pontrandolfo. 2014. Investigating judicial phraseology with cospe: a contrastive corpus-based study. In Claudio Fantinuoli & Federico Zanettin (eds.), *New directions in corpus-based translation studies*, 119–137. Berlin: Language Science Press familiarity with the genre structures – or "generic" structures in Hasan's (1978) terms – through which legal institutions conduct their affairs. Hatim & Mason (1990: 190) use the term "routines" to describe "those conventions which translators either know or simply do not know: frozen patterns of a formulaic nature which are typical of legal texts and which can be translated only resorting to parallel routines in the target language". As a matter of fact, even the most skilled translator may run the risk of producing a translation that is inaccurate from the standpoint of the "register choices", all other aspects of the target text being perfectly acceptable (grammar, content, etc.) (see Garzone 2007: 218–219).

The current studies of phraseology in specialised registers acknowledge the need for corpus-based studies of the prototypical lexico-grammatical patternings and discourse functions of lexical phrases across disciplines. Gaining control of a new language or register requires, following Hyland (2008: 5), a sensitivity to expert users' preferences for certain sequences of words over others that might seem equally possible.

In line with these preliminary remarks, the study stems from three main considerations:

1. Judgments represent a fertile ground for the study of phraseology: the frequent use of phraseological units is one of the most striking features of these judicial texts, a real "trademark" of legal texts (Mortara Garavelli 2001: 154);

2. Phraseology is one of the main obstacles legal translators have to tackle in their professional activity (see Garzone 2007; Kjær 2007);

3. Confronted with the task of translating legal texts, professional translators have few phraseological resources at their disposal.

The relation between "phraseology", "judicial texts" and "translation" appears to have been scarcely investigated so far. The research has represented a first, tentative step towards filling such gap.[1]

---

[1] This chapter is based on a PhD research project conducted on specialised phraseologies employed in criminal judgments (Pontrandolfo 2013b). The PhD thesis entitled "La fraseología en las sentencias penales: un estudio contrastivo español, italiano, ingles basado en corpus" (Supervisor: Helena Lozano Miralles; Co-supervisors: Emilio Ortega Arjonilla, Mitja Gialuz) was defended by the author on 12/04/2013 at the University of Trieste within the XXV PhD cycle in Interpreting and Translation Studies (coordinator: Federica Scarpa). The contribution is also based on a conference paper given during the 19th European Symposium on Languages for Special Purposes, 8–10 July 2013 held at the University of Vienna. It is part of the research project

2 Theoretical background

Phraseology in legal and judicial language is a rather unexplored field of study. The following literature survey of the relevant sources, concepts and definitions is structured into three main parts:

1. Phraseology. A number of influential classifications of phraseological units have been analysed in LGP (from the seminal work of Benson, Benson & Ilson 1997; Corpas Pastor 1996; Gläser 1994/1995; 1998; Ruiz Gurillo 1997; Cowie 1988; 2001; Mel'čuk 1998; Moon 1998; Burger 1998; Granger & Paquot 2008), LSP (L'Homme 2000; Lorente 2001; Tercedor Sánchez 1999; Montero Martínez 2002; Bevilacqua 2004; Aguado de Cea 2007) and legal phraseology (Kjær 1990a; 1990b);

2. Corpora for the study of legal and judicial language (see Pontrandolfo 2012). After presenting the main definitions and concepts, the review focuses on the main corpora built in Spain (e.g. JUD-GENTT, the IULA's COR-PUS, CLUVI), Italy (e.g. BoLC, CORIS/CODIS, CADIS), England and Wales (e.g. Cambridge Corpus of Legal English, HOLJ Corpus, Proceedings of the Old Bailey), as well as in the European Union and the rest of the world;

3. Studies carried out by researchers from different areas and schools dealing with the topic of the present research, as the subject or a side aspect of their investigations.

As far as the third part is concerned, research in this area can be classified into four different subareas, according to the methodological approach, the types of phraseological units investigated as well as the focus of the analysis:

a) Studies that analyse lexico-syntactic combinations in legal language, with a preference for specialized collocations, based on the traditional notion of phraseology (Benson, Benson & Ilson 1997; Hausmann 1989; Corpas Pastor 1996; Berdychowska 1999; Nardon-Schmid 2002; Lombardi 2004; Rovere 1999; Nystedt 2000; Martínez & Soledad 2002; Giráldez Ceballos-Escalera 2007; Anderson 2006; Assunção & Raquel 2007; Biel 2011; Bhatia 2004);

---

titled "Elaboración de una subontología terminológica (español, inglés e italiano) a partir de FunGramKb: cooperación internacional en materia penal (terrorismo y crimen organizado)", whose lead researcher is Ángel Miguel Felices Lago (University of Granada), funded by the Spanish Ministry of Science and Innovation (code: FFI2010-15983/FILO).

b) Studies that focus on the formulaic nature of legal language in terms of routine formulae (Rega 2000; Bachmann 2000; Monzó 2001; Carvalho Fonseca 2007; Giurizzato 2008);

c) Lexicographic studies aimed at building specialised legal dictionaries (De Groot 1999; François & Grass 1997; Gisbert & Joaquina 2008; Fernández Bello 2008);

d) Studies that adopt a wider notion of phraseology and are based on large corpora of legal texts aimed at analysing co-occurrence patterns (Mazzi 2005; 2010; Goźdź-Roszkowski 2011).

The survey highlighted a significant gap in the literature on translation-oriented studies of the phraseological nature of legal or judicial discourse, as there are still only few studies dealing with the role of phraseology in judicial discourse from an empirical, contrastive, corpus-based perspective.

3 Aim, scope and objectives of the research

The study deals with the complex universe of phraseology, in its broader sense (see Gries 2008: 6), from a contrastive (Spanish–Italian–English), quantitative and qualitative perspective. Emphasis has been placed on a specific genre, criminal judgments, i.e. "courts' final determination of the rights and obligations of the parties in a case" (see Bryan 2009: 918).

Judgments epitomise the nature of judicial discourse, as they are the most important acts in criminal trials, and represent one of the most striking examples of "living law" or "law in action" to refer to the 1910's pioneer paper by the distinguished legal scholar Roscoe Pound (see Garavelli 2010: 154; Cadoppi 1999: 253). Studying judgments means exploring the language of the discourse community composed by judges. Narrowing down the huge normative subjects the courts are asked to rule on has allowed to focus on a coherent and consistent share of case-law. Furthermore, this has left room for a long-term study that could delve into the correlation between a specific field of law (e.g. civil, labour law, etc.) and the type of phraseological patterns used by legal experts.

The research questions lying at the basis of the study can be summarised as follows:

1. Phraseology is a key stylistic feature of criminal judgments, a real "trademark" in judges' writing conventions. *What is the quantitative and qualitative relevance of this typological trait in criminal judgments?*

2. Due to the different legal traditions (common law vs. civil law) characterising the three cultures involved in the present study (Spain, Italy, and
England and Wales), *does the weight of phraseological units change depending on the respective source country?*

3. Once a selected number of phraseologisms have been extracted, *will it be
possible to establish a comparability between them?*

The main goal of this empirical study of specialised phraseological units in a
specific type of legal genre, i.e. criminal judgments, is that of providing legal
translators dealing with criminal procedure with a multifunctional resource having a positive impact on the translation process and product. More specifically, it
aims at assisting legal translators (as well as legal experts) in developing phraseological competence, guiding them to achieve "naturalness" in writing through
exposure to real, authentic (con)texts in which phraseological units are used.

4 Material

In order to answer the research questions, a trilingual, comparable corpus of
judicial texts has been built, i.e. the Corpus of Criminal Judgments (*COrpus de
Sentencias PEnales*, COSPE). The focus has been placed on a single genre (criminal
judgments) for a number of reasons (see Pontrandolfo 2013b: 171–181). Among
them, the importance of this specific genre in judicial discourse – see the importance of the judicial "precedent" in the common-law as well as civil-law traditions
– and, from a practical point of view, the need to find a shared ground across legal
cultures to allow for a full comparative analysis.

As Hunston (2008: 156–157) put it, "all corpora are a compromise between what
is desirable, that is, what the corpus designer has planned, and what is possible".
Table 1 shows the result of a number of strategic decisions which have been taken
and challenges which have been tackled to compile a balanced legal corpus. As
shown in Table 1, COSPE is made of two subcorpora: COSPE-Sup which gathers
380 criminal judgments delivered between 2005 and 2012 by the Supreme Courts
(courts of last instance) in the three judicial systems, and COSPE-Ap which contains 402 criminal judgments delivered in the same period by various courts of
appeal (courts of second instance) in Spain, Italy, and England and Wales. These
courts have been chosen for being comparable in terms of role and functions.

With a view to obtaining a representative sample of the genre (see Biber 1993:
243), a number of variables have been established to guarantee heterogeneity
and balance in the process of storing and categorising the judgments, as well as

Table 1: Composition of COSPE (Corpus of Criminal Judgments)

Type of corpus:	Trilingual, comparable		
Languages:	ES-IT-EN		
Size:	Tot. **782** txt (**6,036,915** tokens)		
Genre:	Criminal Judgments		
Period:	2005 - 2012		
Purposes:	Pratice, Research, Training		

ES	Court	txt	tokens
COSPE-Sup	*Tribunal Supremo*	100	1,088,770
COSPE-Ap	*Audiencia Provincial*	127	722,177
	Tribunal Superior de Justicia	35	208,619
	tot	162	930,796
COSPE-ES (tot.)		**262**	**2,019,566**

IT	Court	txt	tokens
COSPE-Sup	*Corte Suprema di Cassazione*	230	1,014,224
COSPE-Ap	*Corte d'Appello*	95	357,057
	Corte d'Assise d'Appello	40	629,905
	tot	135	968,962
COSPE-IT(tot.)		**365**	**2,001,186**

EN	Court	txt	tokens
COSPE-Sup	*Supreme Court*	20	428,529
COSPE-Sup	*House of Lords*	30	455,468
	tot	50	883,997
COSPE-Ap	*Court of Appeal*	105	1,132,166
COSPE-EN(tot.)		**155**	**2,016,163**

to ease its consultation and queries: ID number, division of the court, region/city (to guard against diatopic usage), date of the hearing, subject matter (to vary the relationship between phraseology and specialised contents), type of proceedings, reporting judge (to guard against idiosyncratic usage), notes (e.g. outcome of the appeal, final decision of the court, etc.).

Following Zanettin (2012: 105–107), COSPE is a "translation-driven corpus" in that it has been created with applied (translation) purposes in mind and it does not include translated texts, but texts produced in the three languages under similar circumstances and within the same domain. It is also a "web corpus" ("corpus virtual" according to Corpas Pastor 2004: 227) in that all the texts have been collected from the web (from CENDOJ, DeJure, Bailii databases) and were therefore already available in electronic format. COSPE is currently being POS-tagged.

The corpus has represented the test bed for the investigation based on the research questions which have been tackled adopting a corpus-based methodology.

5 Methodology

The study is a descriptive, empirical research which has fully adopted the corpus linguistics paradigm (see McEnery, Xiao & Tono 2006). Phraseology in criminal judgments has therefore been approached through "real judicial life" examples. Extraction and analysis of relevant phraseologisms have been performed by means of concordancers (mainly WordSmith Tools, but also AntConc and ConcGram).

Querying a corpus of large dimensions like COSPE inevitably requires the adoption and integration of different methods, according to the different types of phraseological unit. Methodologies for phraseology extraction vary along a continuum having the manual analysis on one side and the automatic one on the other. Such dichotomy is also reflected in the corpus-driven vs. corpus-based approaches to phraseology, or, to put it in Granger's (2005:3) terms, between the *bottom-up approach*/corpus-driven (an inductive approach generates a wide range of word combinations, which do not all fit predefined linguistic categories) and the *top-down approach*/corpus-based (which identifies phraseological units on the basis of linguistic criteria).

Table 2 shows the methodological moves adopted to extract the phraseological units around the four types object of the investigation, along the continuum corpus-based vs. corpus-driven.

Table 2: Methods of extraction along the continuum corpus-based vs. corpus-driven

+ corpus-based			+ corpus-driven
Complex prepositions	**Lexical doublets/ triplets**	**Lexical collocations**	**Routine/ Standardised formulae**
Semi-manual extraction (e.g. in + * + with)	Semi-automatic extraction (e.g. * + and + *)	Semi-automatic extraction (MI score[a] of a selection of nodes/key terms[b])	Automatic extraction (ws ConcGram and ConcGram 1.0)
top-down approach			**bottom-up approach**

[a] "A measure of how strongly two words seem to associate in a corpus, based on the independent relative frequency of two words" (Church & Hanks 1990).

[b] To identify the nodes of the collocations an innovative method has been followed based on Schank and Abelson's notion of "script" – "a structure that describes appropriate sequences of events in a particular context" Schank & Abelson (1977: 141) – adapted to the context of criminal judgments of second or last instance (e.g. During a *trial* the *Court/judge* issues a *judgment* against a person accused of a crime, i.e. a *defendant* who committed an *offence*. The *appellant* contests the court's decision adducing his/her *arguments*. The Court can allow or dismiss the appeal (acquitting or convicting him/her), (re)determining the *sentence*. The judge explains his/her *opinion*]. Starting from the script, nine key terms have been identified – ES: *juicio, tribunal/juez, acusado, delito, sentencia, motivo, recurso, apelante/recurrente, pena*; IT: *giudizio, giudice/corte/tribunale, imputato, reato/delitto, sentenza, motivo, ricorso/appello, appellante/ricorrente, pena*; EN: *trial, court/judge, defendant, offence, judgment/decision/opinion, argument, appeal, appellant, sentence* – and later scrutinised to discover phraseological patterns.

To retain methodological rigour, a cut-off point of 5 occurrences per 2,000,000 words has been fixed, combined with the multiple-text requirement whereby a given phraseological unit had to appear in at least 5 different judgments to guard against judges' idiosyncrasies (Goźdź-Roszkowski 2011: 110). The extraction has yielded a significant numbers of specialised phraseological units which will be dealt with in the following sections.

6 Results

A quantitative and qualitative analysis of the four types of recurrent phraseological units mentioned above has been carried out. The following sections contain a summary of the findings that, for reasons of space, cannot be presented exhaustively in this paper.

6.1 Complex prepositions

Following Biber et al. (1999: 75), "complex prepositions are multi-word sequences that function semantically and syntactically as single preposition", i.e. "grammaticalised combinations of two simple prepositions with an intervening noun, adverb or adjective" (Granger & Paquot 2008: 44). There can be two types of complex prepositions: N + P (e.g. ES: *encima de*; IT: *innanzi a*; EN: *owing to*) and P + N + P (e.g. ES: *con arreglo a*; IT: *in ordine a*; EN: *in accordance with*).

These phraseological units, especially the second type, are highly frequent in Spanish, Italian and English legal language (see Pontrandolfo 2013a), as can be seen from the examples taken from COSPE:

- ES: *al amparo de, a juicio de, en aras de, en concepto de, a instancia(s) de*, etc.

- IT: *in relazione a, in ordine a, a titolo di, in conformità a, in deroga a, a pena di*, etc.

- EN: *on behalf of, by reason of, without prejudice to, by virtue of, on the ground(s) of*, etc.

Figure 1 shows the quantitative results in terms of total number, total number of patterns (e.g. as + * + as; by + * + of; etc.) vs. number of types (single different combinations such as "with reference to", "without prejudice to", etc.).

The Spanish subcorpus (CospES) presents a wider variety of complex prepositions (159 different types generated by 14 patterns), compared with the Italian

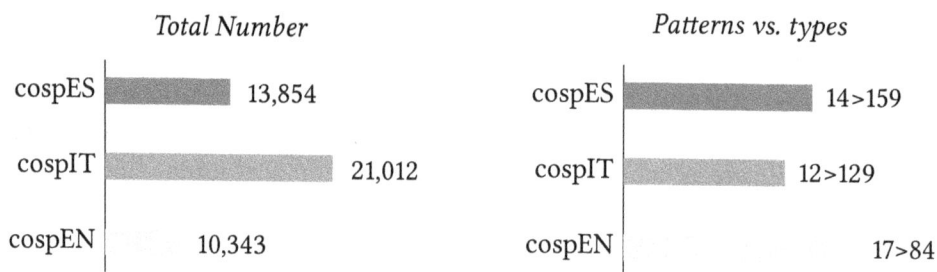

Figure 1: Complex prepositions (N + P + N) (quantitative findings)

one (CosPIT) (129 vs. 12) and the English one (CosPEN) (84 vs. 17). This seems to suggest that, although the Italian judgments contain the highest number of complex prepositions (21,012), they tend to be much more repetitive than their Spanish and English counterparts. Indeed, the 21,012 complex prepositions are always made of the same patterns (12) which compose 129 different types. CosPES displays a lower number of instances (13,854), although the types seem to generate a wider number of phraseological units (159). CosPEN shows the lowest number of occurrences (10,343), even though the range of prepositional patterns is much wider (17), but less significant quantitatively (84 different types of complex prepositions stemming from 17 formal structures).

As far as the qualitative analysis of the results is concerned, obviously not all the complex prepositions detected are typical of judicial language. In order to uncover those phraseological units which are used with a certain preference by judges, a comparison between the relative frequency of these patterns in CosPE and their frequency in reference corpora (CREA and *Corpus del Español* for Spanish, CORIS/CODIS for Italian, BNC for English) has been conducted. "By virtue of", for example, is used with a raw frequency of 26 in CosPEN (normalised frequency of 12.90 per million words), whereas in the BNC it has a frequency of 19 (normalised frequency 0.19 per million words). It is therefore much more used in legal and judicial language. The same applies to "in furtherance of" which has no occurrences in the BNC (vs. 37 instances in 13 different texts in CosPEN). The full list of complex prepositions used much more frequently in judicial language can be found in Pontrandolfo (2013a: 200–cd205).

6.2 Lexical doublets and triplets

Following Bhatia (1984: 90), "binomial or multinomial expressions are sequences of two or more words or phrases belonging to the same category having some semantic relationship and joined by some syntactic device such as *and* or *or*". The following examples are all taken from COSPE:

- ES: *pronunciamos, mandamos y firmamos, [debo] absolver y absuelvo, real y efectivo, natural y vecino,* etc.

- IT: *illogica e contraddittoria, penale e processuale, rigetta e condanna, previsto e punito, connesso e collegato,* etc.

- EN: *adequate and proper, fair and public, reasoning and conclusions, stop and search,* etc.

Figure 2 shows the quantitative results of the doublets extracted from COSPE (triplets do not play a crucial role in the genre under investigations).

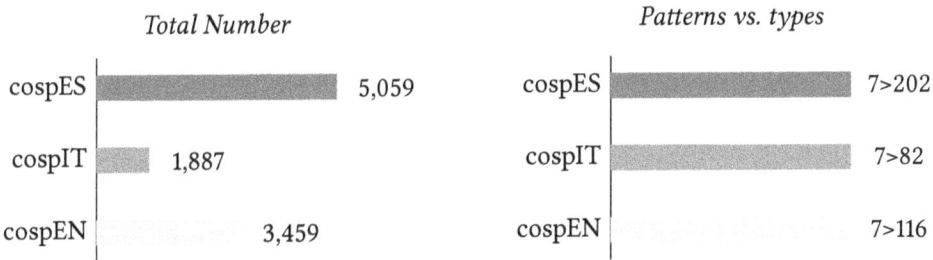

Total Number		*Patterns vs. types*	
cospES	5,059	cospES	7>202
cospIT	1,887	cospIT	7>82
cospEN	3,459	cospEN	7>116

Figure 2: Lexical doublets (quantitative findings)

The analysis showed a proportionality between the total number of instances and the types generated by the 7 patterns identified in the three subcorpora. CospES contains the highest number of types (202) and tokens (5,059), followed by CospEN (3,459 distributed over 116 types) and CospIT (1,887 vs. 82).

The quantitative analysis revealed that the most frequent doublets are those made of two nouns (45% in CospES, 56% in CospIT and 34% in CospEN) – e.g. *violencia e intimidación, contraddittorietà e dillogicità, the prosecution and the defence* – followed by the patterns made of two verbs (22% in CospES, 9% in CospIT and 11% in CospEN) – e.g. *previsto y penado, rappresentato e difeso, aiding and abetting*) – and those made of two adjectives (16% in CospES, 16% in CospIT and 25% in CospEN), e.g. *oral y público, connesso e collegato, noble and learned.* Lexical doublets made of prepositions (e.g. *unless* and *until*), articles, pronouns (e.g. *he or she*) and adverbs (e.g. *before and during*) seem to be used much more frequently in LGP rather than in legal language.

The comparison with the reference corpora confirms that lexical doublets are used much more frequently in judicial language. "Adequate and proper", for example, is used with a raw frequency of 15 in CosPEN (normalised frequency of 7.43 per million words), whereas in the BNC it has a frequency of 3 (normalised frequency 0.03 per million words).

6.3 Lexical collocations

Following Granger & Paquot (2008: 43), "lexical collocations are usage-determined or preferred syntagmatic relations between two lexemes in a specific syntactic pattern. Both lexemes make an isolable semantic contribution to the word combination but they do not have the same status. Semantically autonomous, the base of a collocation is selected first by language user for its independent meaning. The second element, i.e. the collocate/collocator, is selected by and semantically dependent on the base".

The analysis conducted on COSPE has been based on nine key terms (see note *b*) as base of the collocation. As a matter of fact, specialised terminology tends to cluster around terms. Phraseology acts as a link between the term and the text. In particular, the analysis has focused on four types of collocations, exemplified as follows:

1. N [subject] + V

    - ES: *valorar una sentencia, carecer un motivo, celebrar un juicio, entender un tribunal,* etc.

    - IT: *sussistere un reato, ritenere la corte, osservare il giudice,* etc.

    - EN: *plead guilty/not guilty an appellant, hold the court, conclude the judge,* etc.

2. V + N [object]

    - ES: *esgrimir un motivo, aducir un motivo, cometer un delito, condenar al acusado,* etc.

    - IT: *irrogare una pena, proporre un ricorso, accogliere un ricorso, adire la corte,* etc.

    - EN: *to convict/acquit a defendant, to allow/dismiss an appeal, to await trial, to impose a sentence,* etc.

3. N + ADJ

- ES: *motivo impugnatorio, motivo decisorio, pena accesoria,* etc.
- IT: *giudice a quo, imputato contumace, sentenza contraddittoria,* etc.
- EN: *appropriate sentence, reduced sentence, leading judgment, honest opinion,* etc.

4. N + PREP + N

- ES: *celebración del juicio, desestimación del recurso, anulación de la sentencia,* etc.
- IT: *rigetto del ricorso, entità della pena, accoglimento del motivo,* etc.
- EN: *fairness of the trial, decision of the court, commission of the offence, seriousness of the offence,* etc.

Figure 3 shows the frequency of co-occurrence of each collocational pattern, adopting the same categories used for the previous phraseological units (total number of instances vs. patterns).

Overall, the analysis of CoSPE has revealed a balanced picture: CoSPIT contains the highest number of collocations with a nominal base, followed by CoSPES and CoSPIT. The only exception is the N + V pattern which shows a higher number of collocations in CoSPEN (2,084 vs. 112 types).

The most frequent lexical combination in the three subcorpora is N + ADJ (CoSPIT: 4,718, CoSPES: 3,884, CoSPEN: 3,160). However, the total number of types is higher in the English subcorpus (125) which seems to point to a higher lexical variation in English and Welsh criminal judgments. Also the V + N pattern, where the N functions as direct object of the sentence, displays a high number of collocations: 3,774 in CoSPIT, 3,160 in CoSPES and 1,202 in CoSPEN. Yet, a relatively lower number of types of collocations has emerged (CoSPES: 56, CoSPIT: 63, CoSPEN: 43) which could be interpreted as a higher level of repetition or lower lexical variation. Finally, the N + PREP + N pattern shows a trend which is similar to N + ADJ: CoSPIT displays the highest number of collocations (3,519 vs. 144 types), followed by CoSPES (2,717 vs. 102) and CoSPEN (1,074 vs. 42).

A general trend can be outlined: the English subcorpus contains a lower frequency of lexical collocations, which is indeed an important quantitative result (see §7).

The quality analysis of these phraseological units revealed that lexical collocations play a key role in the genre under analysis and significantly contribute to the "taste" of judicial style which translators have to recreate in their target

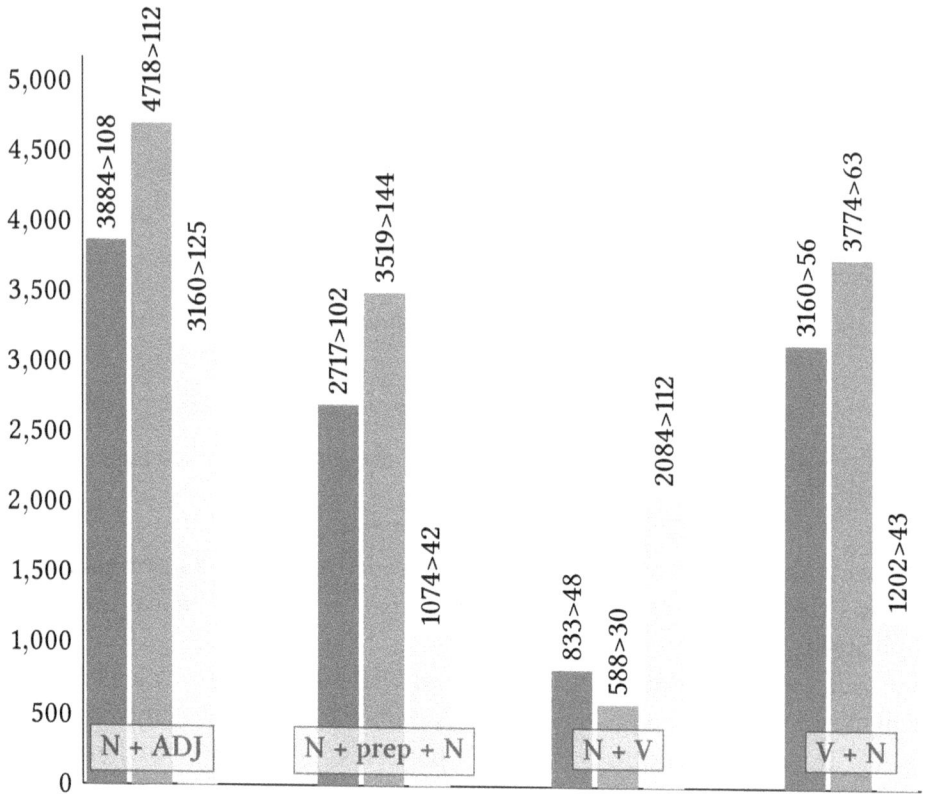

Figure 3: Lexical collocations (quantitative findings)

texts. The comparison with the reference corpora showed that such phraseological units are much more frequent in judicial language than in general language. This is also due to the presence of the judicial term as node of the collocations extracted (e.g. "appropriate sentence" 12.39 in CospEN vs. 0.12 in the BNC; "fairness of the trial" 15.4 in CospEN vs. 0.04 in the BNC; "allow* the appeal" 96.2 in CospEN vs. 1.07 in the BNC). For an in-depth analysis of the qualitative results, see (241–252 Pontrandolfo 2013b).

6.3.1 Routine formulae

Routine formulae or phrases are "recurring lexical sequences, of different length, that develop in the case-law tradition and are usually collected in formularies" (Kjær 1990a: 28–29). The following examples have been extracted from COSPE:

- ES: *Así por esta nuestra Sentencia, lo pronunciamos, mandamos y firmamos; Que debo estimar y estimo; Leída y publicada ha sido la anterior sentencia por el Magistrado Ponente* [...]

- IT: *Con la recidiva reiterate infraquinquennale; Indica in giorni X il termine per il deposito della sentenza;*

- EN: *Judgment approved by the court for handing down; I would allow the appeal and quash the judgment; I have had the advantage of reading in draft the opinions of all my noble and learned friends*

These standardised formulae have been treated combining the insights provided by the genre analysis (Swales 1990, Bhatia 1993). In other terms, routine formulae have been clustered into the five main "moves" of criminal judgments: heading (EN), facts (H), legal background (D), operative part (F), final provisions (DIL). Figure 4 shows the quantitative results.

In general terms, the Spanish criminal judgments present the highest number of routine formulae (1,386), compared to the Italian (740) and English (693) ones. As far as the rhetorical sections (moves) are concerned, the most standardised section of the judgment is the operative part (decision) (CospES: 674, CospEN: 399, CospIT: 324), followed by the heading (CospIT: 353, CospEN: 126, CospES: 53). A high frequency of routine formulae is also found in the facts section of the Spanish judgments (503 instances distributed along 12 types), compared with the Italian (48 vs. 1) and English (18 vs. 1) ones. The legal sections (CospEN: 117, CospES: 87 and CospIT: 4) and the final provisions (CospES: 70. CospEN: 33 and CospIT: 11) are the moves which display the lower number of standardised sequences.

The quality analysis of these phraseological patterns (Pontrandolfo 2013a: 255–261) confirmed that the genre under examination contains a high degree of standardisation and homogeneity, although these two traits do not seem to characterise the English and Welsh judgments. As far as the comparison with the general language is concerned, routine formulae are hardly present in reference corpora.

The following final section attempts to interpret these results in the light of the two different legal traditions characterising the three systems: common law on the one hand (England and Wales), and civil law on the other hand (Spain and Italy).

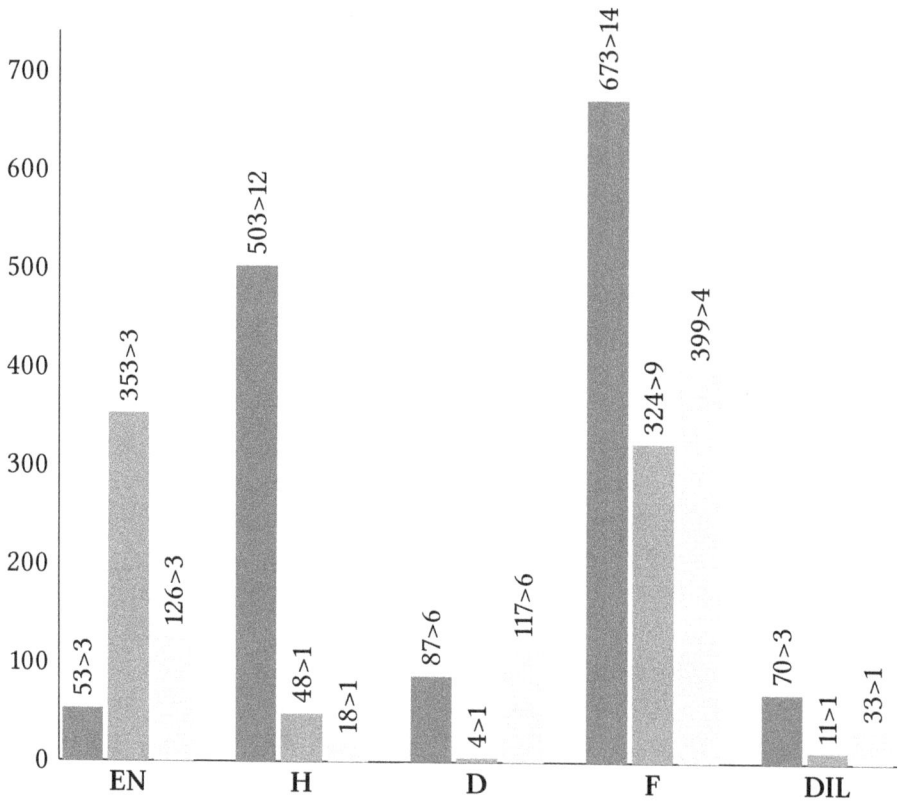

Figure 4: Routine formulae (quantitative findings)

7 Discussion

Results thus obtained have confirmed the three initial hypotheses.

As far as the first research question is concerned, criminal judgments display a high percentage of phraseological units in the three subcorpora. The comparison between frequency of co-occurrence of the extracted phraseologisms and their frequency in reference corpora (e.g. CREA for Spanish, CORIS/CODIS for Italian and BNC for English) confirms that phraseology is indeed a key lexico-syntatic feature of this genre and it is part of judges' idiosyncratic drafting conventions.

As far as the second research question is concerned, the English subcorpus shows a lower degree of standardisation and, consequently, a lower percentage of phraseological units, compared to the Spanish and the Italian subcorpora. As illustrated extensively elsewhere (see, in particular, Pontrandolfo 2013b: 144–145), although criminal judgments have the same function in the three judicial systems, their content and their textual realisation differ significantly. English and Welsh judgments are the results of a long oral tradition. Common-law judges have their personal style, that they use to justify their decisions in a personal, subjective way. There are no constrictions in the outline or content of the texts they produce, also because, unlike the other two, the English and Welsh judicial system lacks important reference texts, such as the Spanish or Italian Codes of Criminal Procedure. This affects the standardisation and the different phraseological weight between English and Welsh judgments on the one hand, and Spanish and Italian on the other.

As far as the third research question is concerned, the results of the analysis interestingly highlight the comparability of phraseologims found in the Spanish, Italian and English criminal judgments. The presence of "parallel phraseologims" is of crucial importance in terms of legal translation. Functional equivalence (see Tognini-Bonelli 1996) can be achieved in most cases, as can be demonstrated by applying the "translation by collocation" approach (see Tognini-Bonelli & Manca 2004; Pontrandolfo 2013b). From the perspective of judicial reasoning, the results seem to point to the existence of a "legal/judicial grammar", especially in the case of Spain and Italy, namely a series of phraseological, idiosyncratic conventions that typically recur in judicial discourse.

8 Conclusions

As far as the applications of the present study are concerned, the specialised phraseologisms yielded by the research can serve, first and foremost, phraseographic purposes, providing legal translators with a practical guide containing useful information on the contexts of use and, above all, the frequency of some expressions (see Lombardi 2004). Such tool will help translators in the stylistic rendering of their target texts and "reassure" them about the appropriate linguistic and legal use of specialised phraseological combinations.

The extracted phraseological units can also be used for lexicographic purposes, integrating already existing legal databases or dictionaries, or constituting the basis for new phraseological resources specifically designed for legal language.

However, the most valuable application of the study is in the training of legal translators. Familiarising with the "routines" of the genre (Hatim & Mason 1997), as well as mastering their use (both at receptive and productive level) are crucial factors in legal translators' training (see Garzone 2007). Phraseology is also a fundamental way for trainees to understand the conceptual relation between the different elements of a specialised text. While terms map out the legal system and therefore pertain to the knowledge (discipline) space in each judicial system, phraseology structures the texts of the legal domain. Getting familiar with the specific phraseology of the register of a discourse community will therefore bring about not only a better knowledge of the genre, but also an enhanced competence in the process of writing and reading specialised registers (see Williams 2002). A tool like COSPE can help legal translators improve their phraseological competence, showing them how to produce texts that fit the stylistic conventions of the target language original texts.

One of the future challenges will be that of enlarging COSPE to include other legal genres, as well as a parallel corpus. This would allow a replication of the study with different legal texts, focusing on a comparison between phraseological behaviours across different genres. Furthermore, a new hypothesis will be tested:[2] phraseology as a quality-enhancing factor in legal translation.

References

Anderson, Wendy J. 2006. *The phraseology of administrative French: A corpus-based study.* Amsterdam: Rodopi.

Assunção, Montenegro & Ana Raquel. 2007. *Estudo das unidades fraseológicas na linguagem forense dos juízes federais.* Universidade Federal do Ceará, Departamento de Letras Vernáculas Tesis doctoral.

Bachmann, Verena. 2000. *Le formule standard nelle sentenze penali di primo grado in Italia, Germania e Austria. Un'analisi contrastiva.* Unpublished MA thesis. Trieste: University of Trieste, S.S.L.M.I.T. MA thesis.

Benson, Morton, Evelyin Benson & Robert F. Ilson. 1997. *The BBI dictionary of English Word Combinations.* Revised edition. Amsterdam: John Benjamins.

Berdychowska, Zofia. 1999. Fachsprachliche Kollokationen und terminologisierte Ausdrücke in der Sprache der Rechtswissenschaft. In Maria Klanka & Peter Wiesinger (eds.), *Vielfalt der Sprachen. Festschrift für Aleksander Szulc zum 75. Geburtstag,* chap. Fachsprachliche Kollokationen und terminologisierte Ausdrücke in der Sprache der Rechtswissenschaft, 259–273. Vienna: Ed. Praesens.

Bevilacqua, Cleci Regina. 2004. *Unidades fraseológicas especializadas eventivas. Descripción y reglas de formación en el ámbito de la energía solar.* Barcelona: IULA, Universidad Pompeu Fabra MA thesis.

---

[2] Future studies will attempt to answer the following research question: What is the relationship between phraseology and the quality of the target text? In other words, is there a relationship between the translators' phraseological competence and the final quality of the text? Can phraseology contribute to improving the quality of translated texts, and if so, how?

Bhatia, Vijay K. 1984. Syntactic discontinuity in legislative writing and its implication for academic legal purposes. In Anthony K. Pugh & Jan M. Ulijn (eds.), *Reading for professional purposes - studies and practices in native and foreign languages*, 90–96. London: Heinemann Educational Books.

Bhatia, Vijay K. 2004. Legal discourse: Opportunities and threats for corpus linguistics. In Ulla Connor & Thomas A. Upton (eds.), *Discourse in the professions. Perspectives from corpus linguistics*, 203–231. Amsterdam: John Benjamins.

Biber, Douglas. 1993. Representativeness in corpus design. *Literary and Linguistic Computing* 8. 243–257.

Biber, Douglas, Stig Johansson, Geoffrey Leech, Susan Conrad & Edward Finegan. 1999. *The Longman grammar of spoken and written English*. London: Longman.

Biel, Lucia. 2011. Areas of similarity and difference in legal phraseology: Collocations of key terms in UK and Polish company law. In Antonio Pamies, Lucía Luque Nadal & José Manuel Pazos (eds.), *In multilingual phraseography: Translation and learning applications. vol. 2.*

Bryan, Garner A. 2009. *Black's law dictionary. Ninth edition.* Garner A. Bryan (ed.). St. Paul: Thompson Reuters.

Burger, Harald. 1998. *Phraseologie. Eine Einführung am Beispiel des Deutschen.* Berlin: Wrich Schmidt Verlag.

Cadoppi, Alberto. 1999. *Il valore del precedente nel diritto penale. Uno studio sulla dimensione in action della legalità.* Torino: Giappichelli.

Carvalho Fonseca, Luciana. 2007. *A tradução de binomios nos contratos de common law à luz de lingüística de corpus.* São Paulo: Universidade de São Paulo. Facultade de Filosofia, Letras e Ciências Humanas PhD thesis.

Aguado de Cea, Guadalupe. 2007. La fraseología en las lenguas de especialidad. In Enrique Alcaraz Varó, Francisco Yus Ramos & José Mateo Martínez (eds.), *Las lenguas profesionales y académicas*, 53–65. Barcelona: Ariel.

Church, Kenneth Ward & Patrick Hanks. 1990. Association norms, mutual information, and lexicography. *Computational Linguistics* 16(1). 22–29.

Corpas Pastor, Gloria. 1996. *Manual de fraseología española.* Madrid: Gredos.

Cowie, Anthony P. 1988. Stable and creative aspects of vocabulary use. In Ronald Carter & Michael M. McCarthy (eds.), *In Vocabulary and Language Teaching*, 126–139. London: MacMillan.

Cowie, Anthony P. 2001. Speech formulae in english: Problems of analysis and dictionary treatment. In Geart Van der Meer & Alice G.B. ter Meulen (eds.), *Making senses: From lexeme to discourse. In honour of werner abraham*, 1–12. Groningen: Center for language & Cognition.

De Groot, Gerard-René. 1999. Zweisprachige juristiche Wörterbücher. In Peter Sandrini (ed.), *Übersetzen von Rechtstexten. Fachkommunikation im Spannungsfeld zwischen Rechtsordnung und Sprache*, 203–227. Tübingen: Narr.

Fernández Bello, Pedro. 2008. Las colocaciones en el lenguaje jurídico. In Carmen Mellado Blanco (ed.), *Colocaciones y fraseología en los diccionarios*. Frankfurt am Main: Peter Lang.

François, Jacques & Thierry Grass. 1997. Les contructions à verbe support en lexicographie juridique bilingue. In Pierre Fiala, Pierre Lafon & Marie-France Piguet (eds.), *La locution: Entre lexique, syntaxe et pragmatique. Identification en corpus, traitement, apprentissage*, 183–198. Paris: Klincksieck.

Garavelli, Mario. 2010. I giudici e il linguaggio. In Jacqueline Visconti (ed.), *Lingua e Diritto. Livelli di Analisi*, 97–101. Milano: LED.

Garzone, Giuliana. 2007. Osservazioni sulla didattica della traduzione giuridica. In Patrizia Mazzotta & Laura Salmon (eds.), *Tradurre le microlingue scientifico-professionali. Riflessioni teoriche e proposte didattiche*, 194–238. Turin: UTET.

Giráldez Ceballos-Escalera, Joaquín. 2007. *Las colocaciones léxicas en el lenguaje jurídico del derecho civil francés*. UNED Tesis doctoral. http://eprints.ucm.es/8061/1/T29838.pdf[05/06/2014].

Gisbert, Valero & María Joaquina. 2008. Consideraciones sobre el tratamiento de la fraseología especializada en los diccionarios bilingües español/italiano actuales. In Carmen Navarro (ed.), *Terminología, traducción y comunicación especializada. Homenaje a Amelia de Irazazábal. Actas del Congreso Internacional 11-12 de octubre 2007*, 211–229. Verona: Edizioni Fiorini.

Giurizzato, Antonella. 2008. Dificultad de reformulación de las formulas fraseológicas y léxicas en la traducción legal del inglés al español. In Carmen Navarro (ed.), *Terminología, Traducción y Comunicación especializada. Homenaje a Amelia de Irazazábal*, 231–246. Actas del Congreso Internacional 11-12 de octubre 2007. Verona: Edizioni Fiorini.

Gläser, Rosemarie. 1994/1995. Relations between phraseology and terminology with special reference to English. *ALFA* 7/8. 41–60.

Gläser, Rosemarie. 1998. The stylistic potential of phraseological units in the light of genre analysis. In Anthony P. Cowie (ed.), *Phraseology. Theory, Analysis, and Applications*, 125–143. Oxford: Clarendon Press.

Goźdź-Roszkowski, Stanislaw. 2011. *Patterns of linguistic variation in american legal English*. Frankfurt am Main: Peter Lang.

Granger, Sylviane. 2005. Pushing back the limits of phraseology: How far can we go? In Christelle Cosme, Céline Gouverneur, Fanny Meunier & Magali Paquot (eds.), *Proceedings of Phraseology 2005. An Interdisciplinary Conference*, 165–168. Louvain-la-Neuve: Université Catholique de Louvain.

Granger, Sylviane & Magali Paquot. 2008. Disentangling the phraseological Web. In Sylviane Granger & Fanny Meunier (eds.), *Phraseology: An Interdisciplinary Perspective*, 27–49. Amsterdam: John Benjamins.

Gries, Stefan Th. 2008. Phraseology and linguistic theory: A brief survey. In Sylviane Granger & Fanny Meunier (eds.), *Phraseology: An Interdisciplinary Perspective*, 3–25. Amsterdam: John Benjamins.

Hasan, Ruqaiya. 1978. Text in the systemic-functional model. In Wolfgang U. Dressler (ed.), *Current trends in textlinguistics*, 228–246. Berlin: de Gruyter.

Hatim, Basil & Ian Mason. 1990. *Discourse and the translator*. Harlow: Longman.

Hatim, Basil & Ian Mason. 1997. *The translator as communicator*. London: Routledge.

Hausmann, Franz Josef. 1989. Le dictionnaire des collocations – Critères de son organisation. In Norbert Greiner, Joachim Kornelius & Giovanni Rovere (eds.), *Texte und Kontexte in Sprachen und Kulturen. Festschrift für Jörn Albrecht*, 121–139. Trier: Wissenschaftlicher Verlag.

Hunston, Susan. 2008. Collection strategies and design decisions. In Anke Lüdeling & Merja Kyotö (eds.), *Corpus linguistics: An international handbook (vol. 1)*, 154–168. Berlin: de Gruyter.

Hyland, Ken. 2008. As can be seen: Lexical bundles and disciplinary variation. *English for Specific Purposes* 27. 4–21.

Kjær, Anne-Lise. 1990a. Context-conditioned word combinations in legal language. *Terminology Science and Research, Journal of the International Institute of Terminology Research – IITF* 1(1-2). 21–32.

Kjær, Anne-Lise. 1990b. Phraseology research - state-of-the-art: Methods of describing word combinations in language for specific purposes. *Terminology Science and Research, Journal of the International Institute of Terminology Research – IITF* 1(1-2). 3–20.

Kjær, Anne-Lise. 2007. Phrasemes in legal texts. In Harald Burger (ed.), *Phraseologie/Phraseology. Ein internationales Handbuch zeitgenössischer Forschung / An International Handbook of Contemporary Research. Vol. i-ii*, 506–516. Berlin: de Gruyter.

Lombardi, Alessandra. 2004. *Collocazioni e linguaggio giuridico. Proposte per un'analisi semi-automatica delle unità complesse in testi del diritto penale italiano e tedesco*. Milano: EDUCatt Università Cattolica.

Lorente, Mercedes. 2001. Terminología y fraseología especializada: del léxico a lasintaxis. In Gloria Guerrero (ed.). Málaga: Terminología.

L'Homme, Marie-Claude. 2000. Understanding specialized lexical combinations. *Terminology. International Journal of Theoretical and Applied Issues in Specialized Communication* 6(1). 89–110.

Martínez, Cruz & María Soledad. 2002. La colocación léxica y gramatical en el proceso penal inglés. *Ibérica* 4. 129–143.

Mazzi, Davide. 2005. 'grounds' and 'Reasons': Argumentative keywords in judicial texts. *Linguistica e Filologia* 20. 157–178.

Mazzi, Davide. 2010. This argument fails for two reasons... A linguistic analysis of judicial evaluation strategies in US Supreme Court judgments'. *International Journal for the Semiotics of Law* 23(4). 373–385.

McEnery, Tony, Richard Xiao & Yukio Tono. 2006. *Corpus-based language studies: An advanced resource book*. London: Routledge.

Mel'čuk, Igor. 1998. Collocations and lexical functions. In Anthony P. Cowie (ed.), *Phraseology. Theory, analysis, and applications*, 23–53. Oxford: Clarendon Press.

Montero Martínez, Silvia. 2002. *Estructuración conceptual y formalización terminográfica de frasemas en el subdominio de la oncología*. Universidad de Valladolid Tesis Doctoral. http://elies.rediris.es/elies19/[14/01/2014].

Monzó, Esther. 2001. Estudi fraseològic de fórmules jurídiques dins de l'àmbit legislatiu. In V. Salvador & A. Piquer (eds.), *El discurs prefabricat. Estudis de fraseologia teòrica i aplicada*, 343–354. Castelló de la Plana: Universitat Jaume I.

Moon, Rosamund. 1998. Frequencies and forms of phrasal lexemes in English. In Anthony P. Cowie (ed.), *Phraseology. Theory, analysis, and applications*, 145–160. Oxford: Clarendon Press.

Mortara Garavelli, Bice. 2001. *Le parole e la giustizia. Divagazioni grammaticali e retoriche su testi giuridici italiani*. Torino: Einaudi.

Nardon-Schmid, Erika. 2002. Lessico e fraseologia nella contrattualistica tedesca: analisi e proposte didattiche. In Erika L. Schena & R. Snel Trampus (eds.), *Traduttori e giuristi a confronto. Interpretazione traducente e comparazione del discorso giuridico. vol. ii*, 167–204. Bolonia: CLUEB.

Nystedt, Jane. 2000. L'italiano nei documenti della CEE: le sequenze di parole. In Daniela Veronesi (ed.), *Linguistica giuridica italiana e tedesca. Atti del convegno di studi. Linguistica giuridica italiana e tedesca: obiettivi, approcci, risultat*, 273–284. Padua: Unipress.

Pontrandolfo, Gianluca. 2012. Legal corpora: An overview. *RITT (International Journal of Translation)* 14. Trieste, 121–136.

Pontrandolfo, Gianluca. 2013a. La fraseología como estilema del lenguaje judicial: el caso de las locuciones prepositivas desde una perspectiva contrastiva. In

Luisa Chierichetti & Giovanni Garofalo (eds.), *Discurso profesional y lingüística de corpus. Perspectivas de investigación.* Bergamo: CELSB.

Pontrandolfo, Gianluca. 2013b. *La fraseología en las sentencias penales: un estudio contrastivo español, italiano, inglés basado en corpus.* Trieste: University of Trieste Unpublished PhD thesis. http://www.openstarts.units.it/dspace/handle/10077/8590?mode=full[14/02/2014].

Rega, Lorenza. 2000. Aspetti e problemi della traduzione delle formule di rito nell'ambito giuridico italo-tedesco. In Daniela Veronesi (ed.), *Linguistica italiana e tedesca. Rechtslinguistik des Deutschen und Italienischen,* 449–457. Padova: Unipress.

Rovere, Giovanni. 1999. Gradi di lessicalizzazione nel linguaggio giuridico. *Studi di linguistica teorica e applicata* 28(2). 295–412.

Ruiz Gurillo, Leonor. 1997. *Aspectos de la fraseología teórica española.* Valencia: Universidad de Valencia.

Schank, Robert C. & Robert P. Abelson. 1977. *Scripts, plans, goals and understanding: an inquiry into human knowledge structures.* Hillsdale, N. J.: Lawrence Erlbaum.

Tercedor Sánchez, Maribel. 1999. *La fraseología en el lenguaje biomédico: análisis desde las necesidades del traductor.* Granada: Universidad de Granada Tesis Doctoral. http://elies.rediris.es/elies6/index.html#indice[14/01/2014].

Tognini-Bonelli, Elena. 1996. Translation equivalence in a corpus linguistics framework. *International Journal of Lexicography. Special Issue on Corpora in Multilingual Lexicography* 9(3). 197–217.

Tognini-Bonelli, Elena & Elena Manca. 2004. Welcome children, pets and guests: Towards functional equivalence in the languages of 'agriturismo' and 'farmhouse holidays'. *TRADTERM* 10. 295–312.

Williams, Geoffrey. 2002. In search of representativity in specialised corpora: Categorisation through collocation. *International Journal of Corpus Linguistics* 7(1). 43–64.

Zanettin, Federico. 2012. *Translation-driven corpora: Corpus resources for descriptive and applied translation studies.* Manchester: St. Jerome Publishing.

Name index

Language index

Subject index

Subject index

www.ingramcontent.com/pod-product-compliance
Lightning Source LLC
Chambersburg PA
CBHW080544110426
42813CB00006B/1203